Best of Luck

HOW TO SURVIVE AS A SECOND WIFE

Maggie Drummond

Illustrated by Peter Maddocks

Robson Books

To my long-suffering husband, Michael Walters, who once remarked that one way to survive as a second wife was not to write a book about it.

To Roger for help with legal aspects
To Dick Allen, Yvonne Moffat and Elke Day
To my friends, Lorna Bourke and Margaret Stone for their advice and encouragement

THIS PAPERBACK EDITION FIRST PUBLISHED IN GREAT BRITAIN IN 1982 BY ROBSON BOOKS LTD., BOLSOVER HOUSE, 5-6 CLIPSTONE STREET, LONDON W1P 7EB. ORIGINALLY PUBLISHED IN HARDBACK BY ROBSON BOOKS IN 1981

Drummond, Maggie
How to survive as a second wife.
1. Marriage—Anecdotes, facetiae, satire, etc.
I. Title
306.8 HQ518

ISBN 0 86051 139 1 HB
ISBN 0 86051 175 8 PB

Printed in Hungary

CONTENTS

USEFUL ADDRESSES

Campaign for Justice in Divorce is a pressure group seeking reform of the laws of maintenance.

Campaign for Justice in Divorce
Coombe House
Butlers' Cross
Wendover, Aylesbury BUCKS

Families Need Fathers is concerned with the problems of maintaining relationships between children and both their parents following divorce and separation.

Families Need Fathers
37 Carden Road
London SE15 3UB

Look Before You Leap

WHAT IS YOUR IDEA of marriage? Open any woman's magazine and you will find the ideal dewy-eyed bride and her eager escort. Young and in love they trot down the aisle with only each other and their mortgage to think about.

The reality, however, is rather different for many couples these days. Each year nearly a quarter of a million people who take the plunge do so by marrying someone who has been wed before, or by marrying for the second time themselves. Nearly one marriage in three involves at least one battle-scarred veteran coming up for the second time. Divorce may well rank as the biggest social upheaval of the Seventies, but second marriage must now come a close runner-up. Once regarded as an extravagant oddity, the habit of Hollywood filmstars or tottering dynasties in search of an heir, second marriage is now, if not the norm, then at least quite normal.

Second marriage was what the Divorce Reform Act 1969 was really all about. A key argument used by Sixties reformers was the plight of the multitude of mistresses and children condemned to living in sin—not nearly so fashionable then as it is now—by the old laws.

Until 1971 only a 'wronged' spouse could get a divorce. Many punished their erring mate not by divorcing him or her but by *not* divorcing. When the law changed, enabling people to divorce even the most tenacious of partners, there was a rush from old marriages to new. The reformers expected the tidal wave to subside after a few years once the backlog of cases had been dealt with, but the continuing popularity of divorce has been irrefutable. Between 1970 and 1972, in the immediate aftermath of the Act, divorces doubled to 110,000. But the number of divorces has just gone up and up—in 1980 there were 148,000.

None of this seems to have dented the popularity of marriage, not at least among the divorced. Over half divorced men, for instance, and nearly as many divorced women remarry within five years. One false start does not put people off. In 1970, less than one marriage in eight was a remarriage, and half of those involved a widow or widower. By 1979, one in three was a remarriage for at least one of the partners.*

And it is not just the remarriers or their spouses who are concerned. There are a host of ex-wives and ex-husbands trail-

* *Divorce and Remarriage: a record linkage study. Population Trends 16 Summer 1979* (Office of Population Censuses and Surveys)

... trailing in their wake a Malthusian army of step-parents and absent parents, half-brothers and sisters...

ing in their wake a Malthusian army of step-parents and absent parents, half-brothers and sisters—a whole swathe of people whose lives are touched by the breakdown of a marriage and the attempt to start again.

However, it is divorce and not remarriage that has grabbed most of the headlines. Planning the future may be less dramatic than debating the disaster but it is no less important. The evidence is that divorce is often just a formal sign that remarriage is on the way. One in three divorced men, for example, is thought to remarry within a year of cutting the knot.* Love at first sight can hardly be that common among matrimony's walking wounded.

Whether you are hoping that love will be lovelier the second time around or taking the plunge for the first time with someone who has tried and failed—the emotional, legal and financial framework of a second marriage may be very different.

How to Survive as a Second Wife looks at remarriage from a woman's point of view. A second wife is in a very different position from a first wife—and from a second husband. Under the present divorce laws, second wives are not real wives unless the first is dead or remarried. Once a man signs on the dotted line to wed a divorcee her first marriage is well and truly over. She becomes his responsibility. But until then she is, in law, the responsibility of her first husband who, if remarried, finds he has to support two families. That men should support their children is a reasonable expectation. That they should keep their ex-wives for ever more is not. Much of the discontent with our present divorce law centres on the anomalous position of a second wife and the absurdity of a system that encourages remarriage but reduces the capacity to pay for it.

The Law Commission's recent discussion paper *The Financial Consequences of Divorce* recognizes the problem. 'The burden of continuing to provide for a first wife can involve financial deprivation for a man who does not remarry, but the burden may well be acute if he remarries and has a second family . . . from the point of view of a husband's second family

* *Divorce and Remarriage*

the freedom which he is given to remarry on divorce (which he might himself not then have wanted) might appear to be nothing more than a snare and a delusion.'*

Whatever the rights and wrongs of the maintenance laws, it pays a second wife to be aware of her position in advance. Most do not realize that their own money may be up for grabs in the current state of the law. Second wives can find all sorts of hands poking into their pockets. No one has solved the problem of keeping two average families on one average income, and coming to terms with the emotional demands of second marriage may be just as difficult. Despite the reality of growing numbers of step-families the amount of advice on divorce contrasts with the paucity of guidance on remarriage. Contrast the weight of wordage on rearing children with the lack of help on how to treat your step-children. Today's second wife may be less worried about how to handle her mother-in-law than about coping with her husband's ex-wife, his friends and his children.

One of the reasons for the deafening silence on the issues of remarriage and step-families is that the Establishment—the Church, Parliament, and even the weekly agony aunts, are still in theory opposed to divorce although in everyday life there is little social stigma attached to it. The recommendations of the Finer Report 1974 on one-parent families, which highlighted the economic consequences of a rising divorce rate, have been largely ignored by successive governments.

Over the past couple of years there has been a noticeable shift away from the free and easy attitudes of the mid-1970s. Even those who a decade ago were arguing that nothing was worse than keeping two people shackled together when one or both wanted their freedom, now think that the cure could be worse than the disease. A few years back the fashionable notion was that parents who quarrelled were worse, from a child's point of view, than parents who divorced. The idea that couples stayed together for the sake of the children was given the sociological elbow. Now the argument has come full circle.

* Law Commission No. 103, October 1980

Mia Kellmer Pringle of the National Children's Bureau suggested that parents should stick to a marriage contract for a minimum of fifteen years. One recent study of the effects of divorce on children has a middle-aged mother talking about why she remains in an unhappy marriage. 'This resentment makes me hysterical, violent and I end up screaming. At the same time I have come to believe that this is, and can be, a real life normal situation. After all, my friends' second and third marriages have failed after divorce because their hopes remained as unfulfilled with the second and third partners as with the first.' Learning to live with all this, she thought, may have been tough for her children, but not as difficult as coping with divorce and step-parents.*

The sixties reformers thought easier divorce would improve the institution of marriage by giving decent burial to the bad and letting the good flourish. For years few people questioned the assumption that second marriages were happier. Lightning didn't strike twice. In her book '*Step-Parenting*' (Unwin Paperbacks), Brenda Maddox commented, 'Remarrying parents have a great deal to offer step-children: the sight of a happy marriage. Statistics suggest that second marriages are stable, that people are likely to remain in them until they are broken by death.'

A decade after the introduction of the new divorce laws the statistics show no such thing. The evidence is that second marriage is as, if not more, wobbly as first marriage. The first attempt to plot the divorce rate of the remarried was made by the Office of Population Censuses and Surveys as part of a massive but fascinating survey of the nation's love life, *Changing Patterns of Family Formation and Dissolution in England and Wales 1964–76*.

This weighty tome overturned the rather cosy notion that, having sown and reaped their wild oats the first time, the divorced got down to marriage more seriously the second time around. Not only did the figures show the divorce rate was ris-

* *Torn Lives—A Study of the Effects of the Law of Divorce on Children* (Order of Christian Unity 1979)

ing among remarriages but that remarriages were breaking up more quickly. 'It is seen that after each duration of marriage that the previously divorced are at a higher risk than those marrying for the first time. For example among bachelors aged 25–34 who married in 1965 about 8% had divorced by ten years of marriage. The equivalent figure for those previously divorced was nearly double at 15%. The pattern is the same for members of the 1970 cohort although the level of divorce is very much higher at equivalent lengths of marriage.'* What the figures show, depressingly enough, is that second marriages collapse at twice the rate of first ones.

Perhaps one reason why people had always thought that second marriage was more stable was that the widowed displayed better luck or judgement. According to the statistics, a widower under 35 who remarries is scarcely more likely to be divorced after a few years than his single counterpart.

Would-be second wives may, at this juncture, feel like tearing the engagement rings from their fingers. But statistics can be misleading. And these particular statistics may be particularly misleading. Many people remarrying in 1971 and after, had been living together in a state of unmarried bliss for years before the change in the divorce laws allowed them to extricate themselves legally from their old partners and marry the new. So a second marriage that appeared to last only five years may have been a reality—though not a legally quotable official statistic—for many years longer. The widely quoted figure—that 40% of second marriages end in divorce—may not be reliable. On the other hand, the earlier optimism that divorcees pull their socks up and do better the second time around has certainly been dispelled.

The ups and downs of second marriage are uncharted territory. One marriage counsellor ventured the opinion that people feel ashamed and tend not to return for help when things start going wrong a second time. When they fail, second marriages tend to be buried with less than the full military honours

* *Changing Patterns of Family Formation and Dissolution in England and Wales 1964–76* Richard Leete (HMSO 1976)

bestowed on the first. There may be an element of 'I told you so' not just from a former partner gloating over events but from the friends, family and other pillars of rectitude who feel called upon to comment. To lose one spouse may be regarded as a misfortune, but to lose two looks like carelessness.

It isn't surprising that the anti-divorce battalion has been quick to point out that divorce and remarriage doesn't always work. The fact is that not only are more and more people doing it, but there is pressure for even easier divorce laws: the Law Commission is examining the grounds of divorce—many think they should be simplified to a one-year separation period with complete abandonment of the concept of 'guilt'—as well as discussing its financial aspects.

This book looks at the pitfalls and pleasures, the differences and difficulties of remarriage. Firstly, it examines the financial problems—not just the laws of maintenance, but the implications for housing, inheritance, pensions and even state benefits. Secondly, as a part-time, and possibly full-time, mother, a second wife may find this aspect of her marriage very difficult to cope with. And, lastly, what about social situations—how do you cope with his friends and family when they have been used to wife number one? And how do you make sure that you are going to be more successful than your predecessor when it comes to coping with him?

Remarry in Haste...

'WHAT IS HIS EX-WIFE LIKE?' all your friends will be curious to know. 'Like nothing on earth,' you reply.

Like mothers-in-law and maiden aunts, ex-wives have their niche in family folklore. But, if you are contemplating marrying a divorced man, it might pay you to find out what she was *really* like—to separate fact from fiction (her fact from his fiction?). Men are advised to look at their prospective bride's mother to see the shape of things to come. Perhaps second wives should take a look at their predecessors to find a guide to their own marriage from the one which went wrong before.

Why do marriages break up? The list of reasons is endless. Favourite is youth. The statistics show that those marrying before they are 21 are particularly at risk. Sexual and financial difficulties run a close second. Differences in age and social class matter too—so much for the fairy tale where the swineherd marries the princess. But these are really reasons why marriages are unhappy. Rocketing divorce statistics do not mean that any more marriages suffer emotional shipwreck than in the past. Divorce on demand has been an easy target for those who want to lay the blame on something, but it hardly rates as a root cause of marital misery.

Mindful of the extent to which the popularity of divorce has lined the pockets of its members the Law Society's paper,

What is his ex-wife like?

A Better Way Out, none the less hits the nail on the head. Defending the right to divorce it says, 'In the past, it was public policy to obstruct divorce in the belief that this tended to preserve marriage and a home for the children. During this century faith in compulsion of this kind has declined, undermined by the feeling that a restrictive law of divorce, while effective in discouraging divorce itself does not save marriages—it only hides the breakdown. A higher divorce rate does not necessarily mean more failed marriages. The lower statistics for earlier years concealed many failures with husband and wife locked into a relationship emotionally dead but legally unseverable.'*

People divorce because they are more idealistic, not less.

* *A Better Way Out* (The Law Society, 1979)

They expect more of marriage than they used to—perhaps more than it could ever provide. One survey of people in second marriages pointed out the central position that marriage occupied in their lives. 'Remarriage illustrates the close relationship between "public issues" and "private troubles". This is the distinction between the world of work, government, social policy and so on and home, family friends and leisure time pursuits. The "privatized world" as it has been called is a sanctuary where "true identity" is played out. Marriage is often found at the heart of this private realm, where you can "relax", "unwind" and "be yourself" in a way otherwise denied by the threatening public world. Some social scientists believe this explains the high remarriage rates among the divorced. These reveal considerable commitment to marriage and the private world it promises—rather than a decline in the importance of marriage and the family.'*

Those who divorce and remarry several times in a lifetime are frequently accused of treating marriage cynically. The truth could be quite the reverse. They may have such a romantic view of matrimony that nothing ever lives up to their expectations. It was said of the seven times married filmstar, Elizabeth Taylor, that she felt she had to marry every man she fell in love with.

The idea of marrying for love is a fairly modern one. Love used to be subordinate to the acquisition of a dowry, land or even a whole country.

Another thing has changed—the social and economic status of women. Whereas our grandmothers, even our mothers, accepted husbandly infidelity because they had little alternative, the idea of a middle-aged man with a wife in the country and a mistress in town may nowadays be regarded as rather quaint, if not downright dishonest. It is far more likely that the wife will be helping herself to a slice of the action as well—witness the number of well-known women who will never see forty again romancing, even marrying, lovers young enough to

* *Why Get Married Again?* Jacqueline Burgoyne and David Clark (New Society, April 1980)

Women who will never see forty again...

be their sons. Twenty years ago divorce was a scandal. Even ten years ago it was frowned upon. But the combination of the easier divorce laws and liberation has produced a new phenomenon—the aggrieved divorced husband cast aside through, apparently, no fault of his own.

Two divorces out of three are initiated by wives. In marriage, childbearing, working and living, women are no longer, thank goodness, supposed to subjugate self-fulfilment to social codes and do what is expected of them. The idea of marriage as social cement has come to be regarded as hypocrisy. It is interesting to see that France, which has maintained a more rigidly bourgeois attitude to matrimony (every Frenchman has his mistress) has a divorce rate far lower than the UK, the US or Sweden. High divorce rates, then, are a function of social attitudes. They do not reflect the amount of philandering or wife beating, or even absence from church in the community.

Most couples who divorce are very keen to explain why divorce happens—and are very keen to blame each other for the failure. No doubt his ex-wife sounds like a regular Medusa or Jezebel. Be warned, though. As one marriage guidance counsellor commented, 'People do not, by and large, marry monsters. Whatever he might say about his ex-wife now, there was a time when he wanted to marry her. Just as he now wants to marry you.' Few ex-wives are as rotten or blameworthy as their ex-husbands make them out to be. Part of the trouble is that the divorce process is not conducive to soul-searching or self-analysis. Everyone—family, friends and solicitors—encourages the taking of sides, the division into black and white, good and bad. You still hear the phrase 'Well, she was the guilty party, you know'. Even Lord Denning, who has never been shy about saying what's what, has remarked that divorce must be regarded as a misfortune that befalls both, not something that can be blamed entirely on one side or the other. Many unhappy couples go all out to 'prove' the other to blame. The battery of propaganda soon begins to sound like a TV soap opera. Always remember if he claims his ex was 100% to blame for the break up, he is at least 50% wrong.

So how do you discover the truth? One of the frightful things about the old divorce law was the way the gory details of a marriage had to be aired in public if the couple could not agree politely on just faking the evidence. Long gone are the days when private detectives snooped in, around or under marital beds clutching Brownie 127s in sweaty palms. Revulsion against this kind of exposure helped to change the law. In its place came the concept of 'irretrievable breakdown' as the sole grounds for divorce. It could be established by showing any one of five facts:

> Adultery which made it intolerable for the other partner to carry on the marriage;
> Unreasonable behaviour;
> Agreement to divorce by both partners after living apart for two years;

Action for divorce by one partner after living apart for five years;
Desertion by one partner for two years.

Adultery alone is not grounds for divorce. Indeed nowadays it may, both in law and reality, be less of a handicap in marriage than the inability to clean a carpet, change a nappy or make a decent cup of tea occasionally.

The law was supposed to take the bitterness out of divorce proceedings. But, in the average divorce, people are still encouraged to be as beastly about each other as possible and vastly exaggerate the miseries of their married life. Despite the civilized option of two years' separation by consent, over half of all divorces are still granted on the grounds of adultery, unreasonable behaviour or desertion—where one party alleges these against the other. One reason is that once people have made up their mind to divorce (if they have found someone else they want to marry) they do not want to wait for two years. Another is that the law is ambiguous on the matter of behaviour. There is still thought to be some material advantage in having a good moan. Despite the ruling in Wachtel v. Wachtel that only extreme conduct should affect the financial provision in a divorce case, a hard luck story can still get the sympathy of the court. Asked to comment on his attitude, one registrar said, 'I do not pay attention to conduct unless it is obvious and gross, but I do pay regard to it if an innocent wife has suffered. I will see that she is generously treated.'*

Thousands of the couples who divorce each year perjure themselves black and blue in order to get a divorce or vent their spite against their spouses. Unreasonable behaviour can mean physical violence or the mildest personal eccentricity. It is used almost exclusively by wives against husbands. In 1979, nearly half of the wives petitioning for divorce did so on the basis of unreasonable behaviour. Only 13% of the husbands wanting a divorce used it. One husband was divorced for an

* *The Matrimonial Jurisdiction of Registrars* (Family Law Studies Centre for Socio-legal Studies, Wolfson College Oxford, 1977)

. . . an excessive love of carol singing

excessive love of carol singing. Another for keeping so many of his papers in his house that his wife was embarrassed to invite people to tea. What was originally supposed to be an objective 'fact' has become a highly subjective fiction. Divorce is still a contest, and people often come to believe their own propaganda. Many concerned with counselling married and divorcing couples find the current process a real barrier to their clients' reaching any understanding of themselves or their partner. It is destructive and confusing. If you want to discover the truth about his first marriage, there is little point in looking at what was said during the divorce. In two out of three divorces wives present the petitions, but this may have little to do with the real situation. Many husbands consider it a matter of etiquette to let their wives do the petitioning—a hangover from the days when, if you were a wife, being sued for divorce was a serious matter.

Superman has nothing on poor average Mr X. accused of unreasonable behaviour. He plays golf twenty-four hours a day, spends the rest of the time in the pub with the lads and manages an all-consuming amour with his secretary on the side. Even at its mildest, the process leads to subtle changes in interpretation. A wife may say of her busy husband, 'Isn't he marvellous? He works night and day for me and the children.' When she divorces him she may claim he was an ambitious workaholic who never had time for her or the family. Of course he is not perfect. Everyone has shortcomings, but they do not necessarily destroy a relationship. One woman's poison may well be another's meat. Indeed virtues can be more difficult to live with than vices. It can be far worse living with a saint than a sinner. If you are the forgiving type who can show love and tolerance for a fond but feckless mate, you would hate to live with some latter-day Calvin who never gave you the opportunity to display your generous forgiving nature.

Divorce may be no training for remarriage, but an endorsement on his licence doesn't mean he should be banned for ever. What may worry a potential second wife is not so much what went wrong with his first marriage, but whether the pattern will repeat itself.

Far from wondering what the ex-wife was like, you may be feeling that you are like the ex-wife. How many times have you heard someone say of a mutual friend's new wife or girlfriend, 'Isn't she like the other one?' They remark that she has just the same sort of hair/voice/eyes/personality. People do seek comparisons, and the media play this up. When Peter Townsend remarried some time after his love affair with Princess Margaret ended, everyone remarked how similar in appearance his second wife was to her. Years later some unoriginal scribe in need of copy for his gossip column remarked on the similarity of Roddy Llewellyn to Anthony Armstrong-Jones in his youth. People do have preferences for certain kinds of clothes, colours, music, food and drink. It is only natural they have preferences for certain kinds of wives. Gentlemen were supposed to prefer blondes. Those who make a study of these things say that people often marry a carbon copy of one of their parents—or the complete antithesis as some kind of subconscious reaction against them. The parental influence is hardly going to stop at the first wife. The girl who marries a father figure or the man who wants a mother substitute clearly have certain very well defined needs, and it seems quite likely that their boyfriends and girlfriends, husbands and wives will conform to a certain type.

Second wives *want* to be different. They find it insulting to be told they are similar in any way. One second wife, asked if she thought she was anything like the first, said, 'Even if I were I don't think I would ever care to admit it. After all, what was the point in his getting divorced and remarried, if he is in the same situation, with the same sort of person, that he was before?' Second wives want in fact, to be better—hence the distinct lack of charity towards their predecessors (usually reciprocated).

Everyone who deals with divorcees—solicitors, marriage counsellors and marriage bureaux—comments on how often they fall for a similar sort of partner. Perhaps you think you share some of her characteristics. Is it time to make your excuses and leave? Not necessarily. One career woman, in her mid-thirties with two teenage daughters, put it like this: 'I was divorced years ago when the children were very young. I have brought them up on my own. I would like to get married again. My ex-husband was a pretty feckless, irresponsible sort of man and I find those sort of people attractive. Perhaps because I am the exact opposite. If I remarry it is certain to be to someone like that. But I don't believe it is a recipe for disaster. When I first married I was very young and dependent on my husband for money. Now I have my own career. It would be ideal for me to marry the sort of chap who would be happy not to bother about working and stay at home with the kids. I think it might work.'

There are no hard and fast rules on compatibility. Circumstances, as well as unsuited personalities, can be marriage breakers. A baby that cries all night can destroy a relationship. Lack of money can kill it off with one couple, make the marriage for another.

None the less, people compare first and second wives, and first and second marriages. It is only natural. But a second wife can find herself at a psychological disadvantage, even while her husband is telling her how wonderful life is now. 'A second wife is really very vulnerable,' said one marriage guidance counsellor. 'If she thinks in terms of her performance versus that of his ex-wife's she may be asking for trouble. Flattery is really an implied threat. Is he really saying how super she is, or does he go on and on about the miseries of his first marriage?' In a first marriage there are no points of comparison. In the second they can be a trap for the unsuspecting. Second wives find out they are like first wives when things go wrong. What is his response when you burn the toast, ruin his shirt or tax him about something? 'You are as bad as my ex-wife.' There is no answer to that! The man who complains that his ex-wife never let him relax at home, but drove him from the house with her excessively housewifely ways stalks into your sitting-room one night with enough clay to start a pottery clinging to his boots. Your first thought is to say, 'For heaven's sake get those filthy boots off.' But that is exactly what his ex-wife would have said, so you keep quiet. Here lies madness—not to mention a lifetime of hoovering. The ex-wife can cast a long shadow.

One second wife said, 'I get very cross because it gives him [her husband] *carte blanche* to do what he damn well likes. Last night he threw his cigarette into the fireplace. It really irritates me because it's such an untidy habit. But as soon as I said, "Have an ashtray," he turned on me. "I had enough of that sort of thing in my first marriage," he said. "I don't want any more of it."'

Much is made of the divorcee's feelings of guilt, remorse and inadequacy after a break-up. But the 'other woman' in the triangle is vulnerable, too. 'Look what I gave up for you,' a divorced man can say, pointing to his children, home and a large portion of his salary. Many second wives feel under the obligation to make it worth his while. Less dramatic, but rather more worrying, is the feeling that you might be second best. These days wives up and leave their husbands to marry someone else, or just to be free of them. Like the second Mrs de Winter in Daphne du Maurier's *Rebecca,* second wives may torture themselves wondering how much their husbands still

The ex-wife can cast a long shadow

care about their predecessors. Journalist Jilly Cooper once admitted to examining her husband for lipstick traces when he came back from seeing his ex.

But not all comparisons are odious. In one of the few studies done in this country on the differences between first and second marriages, many of the 40 step-families studied were conscious of analysing and comparing new partners to the old. Some evidently realized that a repeating pattern of events was due to them, rather than the inadequacies of others. Writing about the findings of their study in *New Society*, Jacqueline Burgoyne and David Clark said, 'Those who remarry often compare their new partners and relationships with those of their first marriages. Many of the men and women we saw said their first marriages had left a legacy of "mistakes" of performances which they would avoid in future. Some had a continuing sense of guilt and uncertainty.

'As one woman put it, "In fact from time to time I see an awful lot of things resembling my past marriage with Michael [present partner] now and I sort of ask myself . . . well perhaps it was me that was a lot to blame."'*

But the authors stress the economic problems of second families as well as the emotional differences. In explaining the apparently high divorce rate for second marriages, they think it is unfair to assume that those who divorce are more than averagely unsuited to marriage. They conclude, 'Former marriages then, have a continuing influence on the behaviour and values of people who marry again. The remarried redefine themselves and reassess the past in the context of current and perhaps changing material and economic circumstances. Yet the combination of private and public pressures magnifies the problems of second marriage. Expectations may be raised among those who think they have learned from experience. Self-doubt and loss of confidence are the obvious risks. Custody, access and maintenance arrangements with former spouses, the legal complications surrounding the sale of jointly owned houses, the problems of finding new accommodation, all this may place heavy demands on family resources... Clearly remarriage poses problems but to explain a second or subsequent divorce as "divorce proneness" or as some American writers put it "lack of marital aptitude" does not do justice to the particular circumstances and expectations surrounding second marriages.

'Many of the people in our own study were aware of their own personal inadequacies and difficulties. But their accounts of their present marriages show how important material circumstances are in affecting the private relationships created by a second marriage.'

'Lack of marital aptitude', however, is one very large question mark that the second bride must raise against a potential husband. As a clinical euphemism for good old-fashioned phi-

* *Why Get Married Again?* (April 1980)

landering it takes some beating. Asked why they think they can succeed where their predecessor failed, second wives usually fall back on relating the ex-wife's inadequacies. Then they think a divorced husband should have learned from his mistakes. Finally, they think they may succeed in taming him. But a man who has left one marriage can surely leave another.

There is no magic formula for discovering whether or not someone would make a good husband or wife, whether it is the first or the second time around. Any woman who indulges in the notion that she can change a compulsive philanderer merely by marrying him must surely be asking for trouble. That doesn't mean that she shouldn't marry him. It means she should be prepared to put up with it.

The statistics showing the speed of remarriage perhaps highlight the most obvious danger of all. The divorced often feel miserable as bachelors again. This feeling of social isolation is commonly supposed to affect ex-wives more than their husbands; but men can be under just as much, if not more, pressure. Ever since the 1969 divorce law was dubbed a 'Casanova's Charter', people have had visions of cads and bounders shedding innocent wives left, right and centre, and going off with their secretaries. England, according to opponents of easier divorce laws, would be turned into a philanderer's paradise. But nothing, in the event, was further from the truth. One judge has said that it would be just as accurate, or inaccurate, to call it a 'Messalina's Charter'. The typical bravado of the divorced man—'I'll never let another woman get her claws into me'—often conceals the desperate truth that he just cannot wait to get married again. Divorced men often feel even more lonely and miserable than the wives who sometimes seem to have the monopoly of public and private concern.

An ex-wife usually has her children living with her, often in the same house, with the same friends and neighbours. She may be hard worked, but she will not have much time to sit around and mope about real or imagined grievances. The daily business of living goes on much as before. The divorced husband, on the other hand, may have all too much time on his hands. He may find practical problems a thorough nuisance. Deprived of his chief cook and bottlewasher, left to the tender mercies of the local takeaway and the launderette, he probably has far more incentive to remarry than his ex-wife. On one level he wants a comfortable relationship. At another he may be looking for a housekeeper on the cheap. Leo Abse, the Member of Parliament who is pressing for a revision of the divorce laws, once said to me that one benefit of sticking to a two-year separation period before divorce was that divorcees might otherwise plight even more ill-considered troths.

Another statistic that perhaps sheds light on the differences between first and second marriages is that in nearly a quarter of the latter, the man is ten years or more older than the second wife. And rather more than half second wives (and second husbands for that matter) had not been wed before.* The picture that emerges is age and experience on the one hand, youth and innocence on the other. Not quite the legendary vision of Lolitas pursued by middle-aged Lotharios, but sufficient perhaps to indicate that some second marriages at least demonstrate the classic symptoms of menopausal anxiety, the desire of the ageing to recapture youth by marrying it. But second wives may wonder whether they, in turn, will be superseded by a newer, flashier and younger model.

One lady, quoted in *Cosmopolitan* in an article examining the attraction of young women for older men, had done her sums. 'I live with the subliminal fear that Stuart, who's just had his fifty-seventh birthday is going to find someone younger, richer, prettier. He keeps reassuring me that he isn't interested in anyone else, but I can't help being sceptical.' In more optimistic moments she tries to convince herself that 'I'm not going to grow older than he is—at least I have the edge over him. When I'm fifty he'll be sixty-seven and at that age, he probably won't be able to get an eighteen-year-old'.**

Men may think that a younger wife will be more submissive, more in awe of them, their position and their achievements. But

* *Divorce and Remarriage*

** *Daddy's Girl Forever* Linda Bird Francke (*Cosmopolitan,* August 1980) what happens when she grows up and decides she wants to be chairman of IBM instead?

It may be easier to understand why the divorced remarry than why anyone marries them. A second wife who is herself divorced with children may see the practical sense in putting two households into one, and having a reliable breadwinner in the family in place of an unreliable maintenance order. But what about a single girl?

One second wife thought that a divorced husband was 'safer'. By that she meant not that her own marriage was more divorce proof, but that her husband was established—in his career, in his social life and, despite the financial consequences of his divorce, was still in a more secure position than her contemporaries' spouses.

But one marriage counsellor pointed out the dangers and pressures on a girl who becomes involved in the eternal triangle. The fact that the man is divorced may colour her view of marriage. She might regard marriage as a tribute, something to be exacted from her boyfriend as the ultimate accolade. After all, she might say to herself, he married *her* (the ex-wife) so he can marry me. A girl who is involved with a single man may not feel so strongly about it, but if he is divorced it sets up a kind of target for her to aim at.

The pressure may come from the man. With a wife on the one hand, and a mistress on the other, he may want to get his life sorted out. This may be the last thing his girlfriend wants—she may be quite content drifting along in an affair. Divorce and remarriage would take the guilt off the gingerbread, so to speak. Some long-standing affairs seem to fizzle out once the possibility of marriage emerges. One couple who had an affair for seven years while the man was married found that, as soon as he divorced, their relationship started to go wrong. His friends found this appalling—how dreadful to go through divorce and then find the object of it all disappear from your grasp. But clearly the relationship had thrived *because* he was married to someone else, not despite it.

You may wonder what to do about your wedding. One of the treats of getting married the first time around is making a big splash, uncorking the champagne and having inebriated and senile relatives tell everyone what you got up to when you were five years old. A white wedding is definitely a woman's occasion and the second wife may well want one. But while the husband who marries first time around may have been persuaded to take part, the divorced man may well prefer a quick little register office job with no frills or flowers and the minimum of fuss. Doing it in style all over again can provoke embarrassing memories, not to mention delicate diplomatic problems. At least half the guests will be enjoying the rigmarole for the second time around. Are they really going to feel that keen on coughing up wedding presents for him again? Do you invite his family if they are less than approving about his divorce? Should you invite his children? Should you invite his ex-wife?

Some second wives feel their weddings a little deromanticized. Their husband's parents, who may remember toasting wife number one a year or so before, may think there is something vaguely indecent in making too much of a song and dance about marrying you. Just in case.

Your own parents may feel less than delighted that you are marrying a divorced man. An interesting sartorial comment came from one women's magazine which featured styles for a second wedding alongside the traditional gown. 'Normal' brides were expected to appear in full length virginal lace. Second wives were relegated to a short little number in off-white.

But don't forget that it's your wedding, too. Having a 'proper' wedding may be immensely important for your self-esteem. If it's what you always wanted, and would have had if you had married a bachelor, just go ahead. One second wife thought she was doing the decent (and cheapest) thing by having a register office wedding with just two witnesses and no party. It was suggested to her that her husband's ex-wife would be upset if she had a big occasion. She was appalled to discover two years later that the ex remarried in traditional style,

Having a 'proper' wedding may be immensely important for your self-esteem

in white and with a Rolls Royce to match—the full works all over again the second time around.

Part of the reason why second marriages tend to be quiet is the problem of having a church wedding. Fewer than one in ten remarriages take place in church. The attitude of the Church of England is that marriage is a sacrament and cannot be dissolved—or repeated. Now and again it is pointed out how this is unfair on a previously unmarried partner—or indeed on someone who was divorced against his or her will—though remarriers may obtain blessings from vicars in some parishes.

Children – His? Hers? Yours?

OVER ONE MILLION CHILDREN, it is estimated, live in families where one parent is missing, or is not the natural father. Kids inevitably suffer when their parents divorce. Not only that, they often have to adjust to a step-parent. And the step-parent has to adjust to them. Sadly, the highest number of divorces involving children seem to take place when they are 7 to 12 years old. Nowadays, it seems people do not wait till the children have grown up before going their separate ways. Remarriage can often be more traumatic for them than divorce. Second wives do not have the same problems as second husbands who usually move in with their ready-made family. They do not have to live cheek by howl, as it were, with their husband's kids. None the less, many feel uneasy about them. If they were being honest many might say they actively disliked them. Others may wonder what sort of constructive role they can play.

It is easy to see why they are called *step*-children. No matter how smoothly runs the rest of the divorce, when it comes to kids most of us stumble. The extended family is one of the chicest, but certainly not one of the cheapest sociological notions. Couples part. Kids usually stay with mum and visit dad and his new wife at weekends. They have children of their own, she has children from her first marriage. Her ex-husband has

them at weekends, along with his new family and his new wife's old family. And so it goes. The nuclear family has exploded. No sooner has everyone buried the idea of the all-enveloping Victorian family than we bring in the twentieth century equivalent. Anyone involved in the divorce marry-go-round can end up with a family tree which would impress the average rabbit. Two out of three divorcing couples have children. Coping with them is one of the trickier aspects of marrying a divorced man or woman. Mothers feel guilty about remarrying because of them. Step-fathers have to learn to live with them, step-mothers end up looking after them, fathers feel they do not see enough of them. The kids become a divorcing couple's favourite talking—or arguing—point. It all gets inextricably bound up with the problem of money. Daddy is bad because he doesn't give us enough to live on. Daddy's new wife is horrid because she spends it all.

For a divorced father, shortage of funds can soon translate itself into shortage of children—though it can work the other way, too. One divorced mother told a judge she didn't want to ask her husband for money because he might not come and see their son. Fathers can be naughty, too, grilling the children about mummy's boyfriends; spoiling them with this and that because they are over-anxious to please.

Even when couples have a relaxed exchange of progeny, they cannot resist using the kids to needle each other. Mark is sent off for a weekend in the country dressed like little Lord Fauntleroy. Jane is dispatched from the commune for lunch with daddy and great-aunt Agatha dressed in denim dungarees and wellington boots.

The children spin between two self-consciously contradictory life-styles.

Men divorce wives, but not their children. He may feel no obligation to his ex-wife, but a second wife cannot help wondering whether she comes first or after his first wife's children. It is one of life's great uncertainties and there is little to be gained by worrying about it. If there is aggravation between the parents after divorce, it can be impossible for the step-parent. It is easy to forget that children are individuals. Second wives find it very hard to divorce their husband's kids from their husband's ex-wife. They often feel that they do not really like the children at all.

Some divorced fathers make no bones about putting the children first—and this can have fatal consequences for the second relationship. Few second wives can stand the thought that they will always be second best. It is worse still if a divorced dad spends a lot of his free time at the children's house. Some divorced fathers are so anxious to keep in touch that they virtually live with their ex-wives at weekends. This may be all right at first. But when he remarries, what second wife is going to put up with that sort of commitment?

It would be foolish to marry a man like that, only to find you can't stand it. You have to discover his attitudes first, and then make your decision. Otherwise you'll end up hurting everyone—all over again. Some divorced fathers have a very idealistic view of their role. They are anxious that as little should change for the children as possible. They want them to live in the same house, eat the same food and enjoy the same comforts as before the divorce. And they want to be there morning, noon, and night to reassure them that daddy still cares. It is completely unrealistic if they are contemplating taking wife number two. Divorce is one of life's misfortunes. You cannot and should not insulate children completely from its effects. If their dad lost his job, or fell under a bus, that wouldn't be their fault either—but everyone would have to adjust.

Many second wives feel hostile to their husband's children

Trying to live two lives instead of one, he will end up exhausted. His children may feel guilty if his sacrifices are obvious, or may wonder why he divorced at all if they are not. His ex-wife may find it difficult to start afresh if he is always on hand to fix fuses and mend the car.

Many second wives feel hostile to their husband's children. They are seen as competition, an extension of his first wife—

which, of course, they are. Kindly souls have been known to do dreadful deeds when confronted with their husband's children. Gentle creatures who give regularly to Dr. Barnado's can become quite savage over an extra 50 pence pocket money. Tolerant women who thrive on chaos may suddenly become houseproud when their paints and crayons make an appearance. Pettiness afflicts step-mothers and though they feel deeply ashamed of it, they cannot control it. Never let this happen to you. In almost every divorce the children stay with their mother. This is often because it is more convenient for the husband to leave home when there is a break-up. The courts do not have to decide who has the children in the vast majority of cases. Where there is a dispute, they are not keen to move children from the parent they have been living with to the other. So mothers almost invariably keep the children living with them. Few husbands even bother to challenge this, because they are told there is little hope. A husband has to prove his ex-wife is unfit as a mother in order to succeed. He will have to show that she is an alcoholic, a prostitute, a loony or a junkie, to have much chance. Judges claim they are not sexist when deciding these things. But in one recent case—the mother of an 18-month-old baby girl left home a few weeks after the birth—the judge told the father that he had been an exemplary parent, but the child should be given to her mother so that he could get on with the important things in life—like taking a job and earning some money.

People get confused by the jargon surrounding court orders about children. Newpapers frequently describe protracted 'custody' battles between parents fighting over who should take full-time care of the child. Joint custody in this country does not mean that children are shuttled back and forth between divorced parents. It simply means that they share important decisions. Taking schooling as an example, joint custody means that a father with care and control may go and see his son's headmaster and see his school report. Fathers without joint custody do not have these rights—even if they are paying the school fees. Many experts believe that joint custody should be the norm, but only a small number of divorces include this arrangement.

Most fathers do not dwell on the legal niceties of the situation. They are more concerned with the problem of access.

Access has nothing to do with credit cards—quite the reverse. It puts the waiting into wanting. Divorced dads get little sympathy if their ex-wives stop them seeing the kids. On the other hand a good 'tug of love' drama can still make the headlines—and the suffering parent is usually a woman. Here sits poor Mrs X. amidst a pile of unopened Christmas presents, waiting for the day her little daughter is returned. Big bad daddy has taken her off, and the police are hunting him. More often than not daddy has snatched her because he knows it is the only way he will ever see her again. No one spares a thought for the many fathers who never see their children because their ex-wives say so.

Couples are encouraged to make their own arrangements over the children. Fathers get 'reasonable access'. How reasonable it is, or whether it exists at all, is largely up to the mother. If mum lives at John O'Groats and he has gone to Land's End it is clearly unreasonable for him to see the kids each week, unless he can supplement British Rail with a private plane. If he lives a few hundred yards down the road, it would perhaps be reasonable for him to see them a couple of times a week.

A second wife who is working is clearly not going to be able to have young children to stay for the summer holidays. If you have other children, you will not want to have your husband's lot every weekend. If you inhabit the smallest thing next to a bed-sit, it is going to be difficult for them to stay overnight. A second-time-around couple could have three different batches of children between them. Saturday mornings can be like Waterloo station in the rush hour.

What is reasonable access to one, may be unreasonable excess to another. It is bad enough coping with the comings and goings when everyone is being co-operative. Life can become very difficult if parents insist on using their kids as battering rams. Your husband may have fixed access but every time he goes to collect the children for an outing they are ill, away or about to do something else. His ex may blatantly say he is not seeing them until he gives her some more money / returns home / gives you up. The kids may be brainwashed into believing their father is the root of all evil, and 'decide' they do not want to see him.

The unhappy truth is that an ex-wife determined to punish her husband in this way is almost certain to succeed. Some men go through long and expensive agonies in the courts to get access to their children—and everyone ends up miserable. By the time they succeed, the children are usually too upset to cope with it. A woman can be sent to jail if she keeps refusing to let her husband see his children. But she has time, not to mention the law, on her side. The court may ask for a welfare report, and a few more months pass. She is given any number of chances to obey the order. It is very rare for the matter to be pursued to the final solution. Everyone knows that putting a mother in jail is no solution.

Unless he resorts to the courts, there is little the divorced dad can do about it. The welfare and probation officers who look after the interests of the young have enormous caseloads. Their priorities must really be deprived or disturbed children. And once legal action starts, everyone gets wound up. Some marriage guidance counsellors offer a sort of after-sales service, and may help both sides come to an amicable agreement over the children. Or a schoolteacher or doctor who knows both the children and the parents well may be persuaded to try and pour oil on troubled waters. An independent third party can be an enormous help. And persuading people to change their minds discreetly is far better than any number of court orders.

If all else fails, he may have to go to court. If he does not get legal aid, it can be expensive. And that can destroy more than the bank balance. The children, the parents, and any second wives or husbands may be interviewed by welfare officers. Some solicitors encourage ex-wives to make the most extravagant accusations. Since she has to make out the case against giving the father access, there are no holds barred. Compared with second wives, Snow White's wicked step-mother has an untarnished reputation.

If he goes to court he may get defined access. This means that the court decides when and for how long a man should see his children. It can be useful when an ex-wife is being difficult but it is definitely a last resort. It ties everyone down to a regular place and time. Turn up two minutes after two o'clock, and the ex has whisked them off somewhere thinking (ha ha) that their father wasn't coming. Take them back a second after seven, and there will be a solicitor's letter on the doormat the next day alleging corruption of the young by loose late night living. If you get an invitation you cannot refuse, it is bound to fall on a day your husband is supposed to see his children. If he has to take a business trip abroad, he is certain to be away on one of his access days. Defined access does nothing to cure the ill will that causes the problem—it often makes it worse. And if you have to miss a day, it looks as though he doesn't care about the children. Defined access is supposed to stop arguments about the children, but only works if you live by a stop watch. There is no substitute for a genuine desire to co-operate.

What about the effect of all this on the kids? In the days when men were men and most women were wives, it seemed important to have a male/female balance in the family through the influence of both parents. Now many women have babies without being married, or without a long-standing relationship with the father. Bringing up baby on your own has become quite fashionable and the position of dad has been undermined. You hear less about children needing a father. Indeed, there is a body of professional opinion which says divorced fathers should not see their children regularly once they leave home. Children, the theory goes, can only relate properly to the resident parent, and the attentions of the other upset them. Similar reports come from schoolteachers who claim that children who see their divorced fathers seem more insecure than those who never see dad at all. Happily, though, plenty of experts think access is a very good thing.

Much of the truancy and delinquency among children is

blamed on the absent dads and broken homes. Sad to say, half the parents who leave home lose all contact with their children within a few months. Fathers are not as callous as these statistics imply. Many are denied access to their children.

Men are often made to feel completely redundant once the divorce is through—except as a source of cash. Their ex-wives can make real contact with the children completely impossible for them. If every visit is preceded by mother's nervous breakdown, and the kids are subject to her Gestapo-like interrogation when they are returned, their father's visits may do them more harm than good—through no fault of his. Fathers cannot win. On the one hand their broken marriages are said to cause dire sociological and psychological maladjustment. On the other there is by no means a clear mandate for the proper support of access. One book *Beyond the Best Interests of the Child* written by three US psychologists put forward the view that access should be at the discretion of the parent with custody on the grounds that 'children have difficulty in relating positively to, profiting from and maintaining contact with two . . . parents who are not in positive contact with each other'. The Eng-

Access is basically unenforceable

lish judicial system has not taken this thesis seriously and has treated with equal disregard the findings of Dr. Martin Richard of the Medical Psychiatric Unit at Cambridge whose research shows that frequent access to the non-custodial parent results in a happier post-divorce situation for the children he has monitored.

Access is basically unenforceable if the parent with the children is determined to resist. Whatever claims people make that the children's interests are put first and foremost the fact remains that they are dealt with last and in the least time. Couples who divorce have to visit—or one of them has to visit—a judge before getting a decree nisi to say what arrangements have been made for the kids. This is the final step before divorce. The divorce itself could have taken years—the average time is around eighteen months. By the time the children officially enter the picture the die is often cast as far as the father's relationship with them is concerned.

Various suggestions have been made about how the interests of children can best be protected in divorce. The establishment of a Family Court, where the whole divorce—money, children and property—could be settled in a spirit of reconciliation rather than the adversarial atmosphere of a court room was the keystone of the Finer Committee recommendations in its mammoth report on one-parent families. Radical lawyers are keen on having the children themselves legally represented in the present system. It is difficult to see how either of these suggestions will help unless divorcing parents can be persuaded, or coerced, into co-operation in the interests of their children.

The influence of the second wife on all this is discussed in the following chapter, *Mum for the Day*. But some second wives may find themselves in the role of step-parent.

Most second wives do not describe themselves as 'stepmothers'. If they only see the children every other weekend or just every now and again they feel the term is presumptive. They say 'my husband's son' when talking to someone who may not be familiar with the set up. A small number of second wives may feel that their presence looms sufficiently large to credit themselves with the title. One second wife who was very much a part of her husband's children's lives saw as much of them as did their mother. They came to her and her husband every other weekend and half the holidays under a long-standing agreement. Once the kids were at boarding school both parents had the equal amounts of time with them. But though the number of second wives who end up as fully paid up step-mothers is small, it is probably increasing. Not just through the death of the natural mother—remarriage rates among the widowed are lower than among the divorced—but because some mums up and leave the nest.

Facts and figures are few and far between, but Gingerbread, one of the organizations for single-parent families, reckons that around one in six or seven of its members are men. But the proportion of divorced men who get to have custody of their children is thought to be far lower than that. Appallingly enough, there are a growing number of cases in America where neither parent wants the kids. At least it rings the changes on the tug of love drama. With the pressures on women to fulfil themselves outside the home a small but increasing number of mothers let the father have custody. In 1978 some 90,000 of the 750,000 single parents in the country were thought to be men.

The Oscar-winning film, *Kramer v. Kramer,* told the story of one father, deserted by his wife, who ultimately found himself having to fight in court to keep his son when his ex came back seeking custody. One of the central issues raised by the film was whether a father should be considered any less capable of bringing up a child than a mother. In Britain, the United States and most of Europe the conventional wisdom is that the kids are best left with their mothers, even when it is their mothers who have left them. Studies have shown that in 9 out of 10 divorces the mother gets sole custody. The statistical evidence is that only in 6% of divorce cases is custody disputed. And in that 6% the research shows the *status quo* was upheld in 9 out of 10 cases. It would seem, then, that any father who was determined enough to keep his children would be able to do so. But a closer look at the research and individual Appeal Court decisions in recent years suggests a disturbing prejudice against fathers even when they have the children living with them.

Commenting on the research findings in *The Times,* Susan Maidment of the Faculty of Law, University of Keele wrote: 'The difference in contested cases was that more children lived with their fathers; and mothers seemed to challenge such residence with the father more than the other way round. It is certainly true that where the court did change the *status quo* it was always in the mother's favour.' She also points out the differences between the studies of what went on in the courts up and down the country and the decisions that are taken when the losing parent takes the matter to the Court of Appeal. 'Over five recent years it was found that half of all the reported appeal cases resulted in the mother getting custody although the father had the *status quo.* In seven of these 19 cases it was the judge's simple view that young children needed their mother that was the dominant factor in the decision.'* Recent Appeal Court decisions on custody have done nothing to dispel the view that divorced dads get a raw deal on custody.

Men left holding the baby stand a bigger chance of losing it if their ex-wives come back to try for custody. Perhaps it is this insecurity that gives many single fathers their evangelical air and disconcerting mastery of the latest trends in child psychology. Most of them tackle fatherhood with enormous enthusiasm—like a new hobby, job or religion. Single fatherhood is becoming socially acceptable, partly because of the publicity surrounding *Kramer v. Kramer.* Shortly after the film's release the *Daily Express* showed its readers three such dads—on the Woman's Page strangely enough. None of them seemed too keen to remarry, or even acquire a serious romantic interest. Far from feeling they needed to find a new mum for their children they seemed to be thrilled to bits with their new found world of cooking, mending and cleaning. 'As the

* *The Times,* April 1980

children get older, I might have some more time for myself. I might marry again, but I wouldn't bring a girlfriend home for the moment—too unsettling for the children,' said one. There are no figures on what proportion of single fathers remarry but it would be no surprise if it is a lower percentage than divorced people generally.

However a growing number of second wives may still have mothering thrust upon them. There you are cosily installed as his new missus and his ex decides she has better things to do with her life. Most step-mothers, however, know what they are in for at the beginning: love me, love my children—or at least try to live with them. Many women find it a daunting task and no wonder. Step-mothers have a powerful fairy tale image. Grimm was aptly named. But for a man seeking to keep custody of his children the presence of a second wife can be an enormous asset. Faced with a mother on one hand and a father and his second wife or girlfriend on the other more than one judge has decided that the man should retain custody because he has a two-parent family to offer.

Step-mothers may well feel that more is expected of them than of step-fathers. A man who marries a divorcee with children does not take on the day to day burdens of a mum. Single fatherhood is still unusual and the circumstances in which step-mothers come by their position are more often unhappy or bizarre.

Rule one must be not to make judgements about the absent parent—at least not in front of the children. One second wife who had brought up her husband's little girl virtually from birth lamented the erratic interest that her mother showed in her offspring. Birthday presents would arrive unwrapped, on the wrong day or not at all. The mother was a devotee of a weird religious sect which made any normal way of life difficult. 'I think Susie is very disappointed in her mother,' said this step-mum, 'but she is her mother and we try and keep the relationship going.' Many others in her position may feel vastly more self-righteous with far less reason but it is difficult to spend your days cooking, cleaning and worrying for a child who hops off for a monthly or weekly visit and comes back full of comparisons. It is, if anything, even worse competing with a ghost. An ex-wife who has left her children is all too obviously full of human fallibility and perhaps you ought to be grateful. The dead can do no wrong.

Step-parents—proper full-time step-parents—seem to spend a lot of time brooding on what the children should call them. It is a practical problem which conceals a much bigger identity crisis. Step-mothers, even more than step-fathers, know what is expected of them. The unknown quantity is the children. What do they make of it all? Step-parents are not supposed to expect bouquets if everything turns out all right but they may suffer more blame if it doesn't. Step-mothers want to be perfect. But in ordinary families things are not perfect. One solicitor, bemoaning the silliness of the courts in placing so much importance on keeping children of a family together said if he ever got a divorce he felt it would be quite reasonable to share his children out. The boy and girl were always fighting and the daughter didn't get along with her mother. This was a respectable 'happy' family and he just accepted the situation as normal. If he had been a step-father would he have been riddled with guilt?

Nuclear families suffer fission. Step-families may feel under more pressure to put on a happy face—perhaps to impress former spouses as much as anything. But there is no getting round the fact that it is the luck of the draw. When natural parents can make such a mess of their relationships with sons and daughters, how much more likely that an outsider, an intruder, will make a botch of it as well. A natural mother or father can always claim that a child was loved or wanted. But everyone knows that with a second wife—or husband—marriage is despite, rather than because of, the children.

The problems of step-parenting have received scant official recognition. Yet of all the changes brought about by the 1969 Divorce Law Reform Act the bringing together of unprecedented numbers of step-parents and children is surely the most significant. There is much public wringing of hands about the effects of divorce on children, the social and economic problems of one-parent families and the destruction of family life. But little about what seems to be the even more turbulent experiences that can follow remarriage, particularly for the partners who have the children living with them. You can glimpse the tip of the iceberg in the gruesome reports of child-battering cases. A large proportion of the ones that hit the headlines feature the step-father in the role of the villain. A natural father can be hauled into court, have access to his children reduced or taken away if the judges who decide these things think it is in the best interest of the child. But a mother can saddle her children with a step-father who might be a die cast rogue and there is nothing anyone can do about it.

Second wives who have children from a first marriage can be in a particularly invidious position. Unlike the second wife who plays part-time nurse maid to her husband's brood, at weekends the divorcee with kids has two lots to contend with, as well as importing a full-time step-father into the household. Kids do not seem to be a bar to marriage. It was often thought that divorced women with children would find it hard to remarry because a man wouldn't want to take on the financial responsibilities of a ready-made family. If that were so it would be logical to suppose that women with young children—who had to be supported for the foreseeable future and whose mothers might not have the opportunity to work—would find remarriage most elusive. But remarriage samples show quite the reverse. Over half of all divorced mothers with children under 10 years old remarry within a few years.

When two divorced people with children get married life becomes even more complicated. One step-father who married a divorcee said that when the ex-husband in turn remarried a divorcee with kids he lost all interest in his original brood. The situation presents an entirely different set of problems. His children are likely to regard your children as cuckoos in what they see as their second nest. A mother whose original husband had foisted all responsibility for the children off on to her will often try to make her second husband a proper father figure—particularly if the children are young enough to accept him. The dangers of doing this when the husband has a first family are obvious. A divorcee with children marrying a divorced man also with children can be getting the worst of all worlds. No longer regarded by the law as dependent on her divorced husband (although her children are still his responsibility) her arrival on the scene with her expensive brood will in no way affect her husband's obligations to his ex-wife.

In one case dealing with such a group of people on very low incomes a judge dismissed the second wife, a divorcee with two children, with the remark that what the husband did with his money was his own business. He had to pay the same amount of maintenance to his ex-wife. His new wife's children, the judge said, were the responsibility of their own father. Any supplementary benefit that a single-parent family receives is stopped on remarriage, or even cohabitation. If benefit is being paid for the children the state offloads the financial obligation on to the new husband, whatever his circumstances or other obligations may be. Financially speaking, second families become not so much extended as stretched beyond endurance if the new couple decide to have children of their own.

Moneywise it can be a very difficult decision. If you are a second wife who is working you may feel reasonably well off. You may well be earning more than your husband is paying his ex in maintenance. You have your own money and, within reason and the limits of your bank account, you can buy what you want. But, if you give up working to have a baby, things will change dramatically. An ordinary couple will probably find the cut in living standards a baby brings easier to accept. For you, there will always be an additional resentment that he is having to support his ex-wife at the expense of you and your children. There is always the chance that his ex could suddenly get remarried, and a large burden could be shifted. But if you wait for that happy day, when it finally dawns, you may be too old to start a family and you will resent that too.

Perhaps you should look closely at your motives. One second wife, delighted with her family, now says that what had originally made her want children was the feeling that her marriage would not be taken as seriously as her husband's first one unless they had a baby.

Some men do not want children the second time around. One second wife of a rich businessman dithered about having a child for years. She was well into her thirties. Her husband had three by his first marriage and would have run a mile at the thought of more. She decided against and, whatever her regrets at never having a child, she has a happy marriage.

Second wives should be clear about children from the start. Men with one family sometimes do not want, nor can they afford, another. If he was used to coming home each night to find his ex-wife exhausted, the place a mess and a sink full of nappies, you have a hard task to change his mind about the joys of fatherhood. One second wife whose husband had two boys married knowing her husband was opposed to any more. He eventually succumbed and was delighted with his baby daughter. Perhaps she was lucky in producing the right variety. But it could be a mistake thinking you can change his mind about children.

It is quite acceptable nowadays for mothers to work, even when their children are very young. But finding someone to take your place at home is an expensive problem. By the time you have paid someone to look after the children and paid your tax and national insurance it may not really be worth your while unless you earn a high salary. And you may feel angry that you have to go out to work so that an ex-wife with older and less dependent children can sit at home.

How will his children react? Some fear that they are about to be replaced in their father's affections. A hostile ex-wife may encourage these feelings. But most kids are quite intrigued by the thought of a little half-brother or sister. So long as no one else makes too much of a song and dance about it, his other children will take it in their stride. The age gap will probably be wide enough to ensure that there is little direct competition between old and new. Toddlers and teenagers usually get on famously together.

Left to their own devices, half-brothers and sisters usually grow up accepting, even being fond of each other. But some fathers start paying less attention to the first batch of kids when the second comes along. This is unfair. Try to keep everything normal. His children should be able to come and stay as usual. They should not be made to feel they are being shoved aside to make way for newer and more interesting rivals. And do not let their grandparents coo over your infant while ignoring their other grandchildren. Your small baby may be fascinating, but it has far less to offer socially than your husband's 12-year-old. Do not let their own mother put them off. Once they are presented with it, children find a baby almost impossible to resist. Spend some special time exclusively with the older child—perhaps when baby is asleep—and involve them in looking after it.

Some divorced men make much better fathers the second time around. Do not listen to his ex-wife when she says how useless he was with kids. He may not have been a doting father when his first two were toddlers – he may have been too young and more interested in playing football with his mates than rushing round the back garden with his son. This does not mean he is going to be like that again. Many fathers say how much more pleasant and relaxed it is being a dad for the second time. And there can be positive advantages for you. Years of practice mean that a discerning dad instinctively knows the difference between a meaningful wail and a burst of bad temper. He may not be keen to join the other eager beavers at the ante-natal breathing classes, and display bored indifference to your aches and pains, but you may find him a tower of strength with an intransigent infant at three o'clock in the morning while all the novice fathers are having nervous breakdowns along with their wives.

For him, having a second family may be much more of a conscious decision. People get married, get mortgaged, have children, because it is expected of them. It fits the pattern. Second time around he is probably much more positive about the whole thing. But it is very important to face the money problem full on, first. After all, you cannot expect his existing family to cut back on their ice cream and Mars bars just because you have now decided to have a baby and can no longer work full time. If his first wife has older children and could well do something to earn her living, but will not, you

The sad fact is that many second wives cannot afford . . .

may be entitled to view the situation less charitably. How long are the other children likely to be dependent? Is there much chance of his being able to reduce the maintenance to his ex-wife once they are grown up?

The sad fact is that many second wives simply cannot afford to have children and live in a way that suits them. Everyone has standards; and how the children adjust to them does depend on the parents. Kids do not need expensive toys to make them happy—but they are going to be unhappy if their mum is totally depressed all the time and moaning about money. It might be even worse if you have a target handy, like his ex-wife, to blame your troubles on. It can end up embittering your own relationship with your husband. It is too easy to say, 'It's all right for you, you've got children of your own already.' And you are naturally going to resent his children, too.

If you want children you should say so before you marry. You should weigh up the situation to see if you are going to be able to afford it. When people marry for the first time both usually look forward to having a family. With second marriages it is different.

Mum for the Day

ONE THING YOU WILL DISCOVER is that every other second wife you meet gets on with her husband's children better than you do. Or seems to. The truth is that it is not an easy situation for anyone. In an ideal world everyone would remain on good terms or at least try to sink their differences for the sake of the kids.

Unfortunately, divorcing parents often behave rather like children themselves. You may be an island of sweet reason in the hurricane of emotions, but you may find it surprisingly difficult to get on with his children. You may not know too much about children for a start, and the kids themselves may not be at their most charming. You should get to know them properly before you marry their father. Make it a gradual process. Do not make your first contact on a family outing to the Hebrides for a week. Sheep are not much of a distraction for a muddled seven-year-old. Join them for lunch one day, go with them and their dad to the museum or the funfair next time. Have them round to your place for the day. A second wife, or anyone who looks like a potential second wife, can have a disastrous effect on a father's relationship with his children, no matter how hard she tries. An amicable divorce can become decidedly hostile from the ex-wife's point of view once a successor is in sight. If an ex-wife wants to play dirty, you have to be calcu-

You may be an island of sweet reason in the hurricane of emotions, but you may find it surprisingly difficult to get on with his children

lating. If you do not know her already (very few people marry their best friend's mate) try not to bump into her. If the children know she has never clapped eyes on you, she is going to look silly when she starts moaning about you.

You cannot expect them to like you just because you are dad's new wife. That may be one big reason for them not to like you—at first. Many kids try to get their parents back together again after a divorce. They dream of a reconciliation, with everyone living happily ever after. Your arrival on the scene may shatter these hopes and they will resent it. If you are one of the reasons why their father divorced, they are naturally going to blame you for their troubles and their mum's. It might be diplomatic—and better for your image in the longer term—if you do not get to meet them until things have settled down a bit. Your life has enough problems without deliberately casting yourself as the villain of the piece in the opening scene. It is asking a bit much of his kids if you turn up on his arm the weekend after he leaves home.

If he has been divorced for years his kids may be used to the odd girlfriend (they are bound to describe them all to you in graphic detail) around the place. But when something serious—like you—makes an appearance they may start getting worried that, once married, he will have less time for them. They will try and put him off you—'I liked Susie's cooking much better'; and even you off him—'Daddy's been engaged hundreds of times since his divorce'. Either way you may be an object of suspicion.

Do not look on his children as a challenge—something to be won over to your or even your husband's way of thinking. Search for the common ground. It could be a hobby you know something about—a game you both play well or even a television programme you love—or love to hate. Do not get put off if your friendly overtures meet with an ungracious rebuff. You may find, too, that you become swiftly annoyed at small incidents that would normally, with another child, never worry you.

It isn't just a question of irritation at the sheer amount of noise, mess and untidiness that children can inflict on a chic little bachelor pad. It is far more deep-seated. 'When she disagrees with me,' said one second wife of her husband's daughter, 'I feel I am arguing with her mum. I am hardly prepared to listen, let alone let her win.' At root it is good old-fashioned jealousy. Jilly Cooper once confessed how angry she felt when her stepdaughter polished off the last piece of chocolate cake. If anyone else in the house—even the dog—had done it, she reflected, she would not have minded in the least. The second wives most successful with the children seem to be the ones who are either on reasonable speaking terms with their mother, or who have never come across the lady at all. It helps, too, if one side is not taking the other to the proverbial cleaners. One honest comment came from a reader of the *Guardian* who wrote, 'What second wife is going to feel generously inclined towards the children of her husband's first marriage if she knows that their mother is getting a third of her husband's gross salary for life?' Second wives may feel less than kind.

Even if you meet your husband's children firmly convinced that maintaining his relationship with them is *a good thing*, you may find your noble intentions tested to the utmost, particularly if you have little experience of kids. 'When I first met them I thought my husband's kids were horrible,' confided one second wife. 'They seemed to be so demanding. Forever grabbing crisps and sweets and never saying thank you. Of course, I knew nothing about children then and they were as terrified of me as I was of them.'

Many childless women seem to have very strong views on children. It is all very easy when there is no chance of having to eat your own words. Most mums muddle along in a way that suits them. The strictest principles—no sweets *at all, never?*—bend, if not crack completely, in the face of screaming toddlers and awkward teenagers. It is all very well for you to think that his ex shouldn't let them watch television all day, but if you had the job of entertaining them constantly you might welcome Batman, Popeye or the Incredible Hulk into your living-room with a sigh of relief.

Many second wives seem strangely critical of their husband's children. 'Oh they are nice children but—' is a familiar response. If they were referring to nephews or nieces, godchildren or even the neighbours' offspring there would be no need for qualification. On the other hand a second wife will rarely come straight out with it—'They are right little so and so's'—even if they are. They may have no inhibitions about what they say regarding other children.

Asked what she thought she had learnt from coping with her husband's child one second wife said 'humility'. Single women, she thought, found it particularly hard to adjust. 'You learn not to always think of yourself, not to see setbacks as something done to you.' Recognizing you feel a little hostile may be half the battle won. You can make a conscious effort to overcome your pride and prejudice. The important thing is that the children are happy to see their father—not that you lose face, or his attention while they are there. The older children are, the more difficult they can be. Divorced women with teenage children are less likely to remarry than those with

The older children are, the more difficult they can be

young ones. This has less to do with the age of the mothers, more the way older children still at home raise strenuous objections to anyone who looks like becoming a permanent mate. Divorced dads can suffer the Tatum O'Neal syndrome. Teenage daughters, too big for their boots, can object violently to dad's new girlfriend and prospective wife. Few dads are daft or doting enough to allow this to stand in the way, but it is not unknown. One middle-aged man with a daughter of 15 and a fiancée of 30 went all through a divorce, ostensibly to marry wife number two. In the end he had to choose not between his ex-wife and his mistress, but between his daughter and his mistress. The daughter won. Husbands seem to think their young second wives and teenage daughters will get on famously together. Alas, it is rarely so.

An attractive young wife spells competition for a possessive teenage daughter. Her own mother was never such a rival. Youngsters often declare themselves quite shocked when a middle-aged dad is remarried to a bright young thing. The most dissolute teenager starts sounding like a recruit to the Salvation Army when he introduces her to a fiancée who is not old enough to be her mum. Plus the fact that if a parent has been on his or her own for some time the kids may be protective—and more jealous than ever about a new wife or girlfriend. Feelings can run high—and carry on running beyond the grave. Christina Onassis was only able to really vent her anger at her father's second wife, Jackie Kennedy, once the old chap was dead and gone. Battles over wills often dredge up bitter emotions. The money is often just a side issue. Step-daughters sometimes seem an ungracious lot.

Equally second wives find teenage daughters difficult. They may seem remarkably precocious and down-right rude. They are not, like teenage sons, susceptible to feminine wiles. They can be extremely unlovely if they want. Whatever the commercials may say, it is very strange for mothers to look as young as their daughters. How is a nearly grown-up daughter supposed to react to a second wife who may be just a few years older? She cannot treat her as a mother figure—she's already got a mother. And girls often fight with their elder sisters. You are older and more experienced, and it is really your responsibility to make it as easy as possible for her.

She might want to spend some time with her father on her own—and why not? One husband, whose second wife goes abroad a lot, regularly takes his teenage daughter from the first marriage and the two youngsters from the second off for a weekend in the country when his wife is away. When the second wife and daughter are together they fight. He can only enjoy the company of both by keeping them apart.

The last thing you want is for older children to feel they are strangers in their father's home. Do not feel you have to do everything for them—it will just make them feel like a visiting guest. Do not accuse them of using the house like a hotel—they probably get enough complaints like that from their mother. Once children have grown up they visit their parents because they want to, not because they have to.

Some second wives clearly feel that weekly visits from their husbands' kids are a bad idea from the children's point of view, particularly when their mother may have remarried and provided them with a new 'daddy'. It is tempting to think that young children may forget and latch on to a new relationship, leaving their father with no emotional ties. Maybe a baby forgets, but toddlers certainly do not: there is no way of knowing that the new relationship will survive. A father who divorces normally keeps contact with his children after divorce. It is very rare for a step-parent—even if he or she has brought up the children from an early age—to maintain a relationship with them once a marriage is over. One second wife became so upset by all the post-divorce aggravation that she really began to think that it would be better if her husband never saw his children again—or at least only occasionally. Her husband's ex-wife had remarried and all over the house appeared the gooey Father's Day and birthday cards bearing the legend 'To Mark (such was the new husband's name) the best father in the world'. But Mark walked out after less than two years of marriage and only afterwards did the children ever tell their father about the rows and problems of their mother's short relationship.

In rare cases it may be best that a child grows up thinking that mum's second husband is the real father—perhaps the ex disappeared shortly after, or even before birth. Many experts would take the argument further, for instance: 'Some parents feel that they should make a clean break from their children—they think it would be better for them. But they are in fact attempting to save themselves from the pain that the failed marriage has caused them as well as the pain of seeing their children for a brief spell and having again to part. It cannot be stressed too often that such parents endanger the mental health of their children either temporarily or permanently.'*

However, in normal circumstances, the second wife who encourages her husband's worry that he is doing more harm

* *The Rules of the Tug of Love Game* Robin Benians (*Guardian*, 1979)

than good by seeing his children should examine her conscience carefully—is she really trying to make life easier for herself?

If mummy is going to make things difficult you'll have to swallow your pride a bit. 'Mummy does it this way', 'Mummy never does it that way' will be familiar refrains, greeting everything from the cornflakes at breakfast to the way you knot little Simon's tie. Take the line of least resistance. Do it mummy's way, for heaven's sake, unless the demands start becoming ridiculous. You may find it irritating, demeaning even, to bend to the whims of a pint-size critic, but for children, superficial things—like the colour of the gravy, the crinkle in the chips, the brand of the baked beans—are a matter of life or death. Kids are junk food gourmets. And food may be one subject you'll find hard to swallow. 'Don't like stew' is the typical response to your carefully prepared *boeuf bourguignon.* Do not daub it all over them in response. Just give thanks for the local Wimpy Bar.

Do not let your husband become too insistent on the kids having to do things his way, or like the things he likes. The best intentioned dad sometimes gets a little obsessed that his son should be playing rugby 24 hours a day. Since he may see so little of him he feels he wants to put over his ideas more forcefully. This can spell disaster for everyone. The child may come to dread seeing his father because he feels he is going to be preached at. Point out to your husband that tycoons frequently produce sons who become academics, weight-lifters father ballet dancers, and chartered accountants have been known to produce poets. He cannot really expect his children to be replicas of himself—whether divorced or not the end result will probably be the same.

This is one area where you might have real power for the good. Divorced parents are sometimes so busy scoring points against each other that they forget the real interests of their kids. Battles over what school they should go to, what time they should go to bed and what should, or should not, be bought for their birthdays are often just another way for them to continue their fight. Young children are made very insecure if one parent is aggressively hostile to the habits or ideas of the other. I remember that my holidays with my father were completely ruined because he, an atheist, was forever condemning religion while my mother, a devout Catholic, had brought me up in the faith.

However strongly your husband feels about the need to impress his children with the right sort of ideas and values, it is hopeless if he spends his time with them talking like some high pressure salesman. Divorce seems to make little difference as to whether children accept or reject their parents' beliefs. Time and time again they do something completely different. Ronald Reagan hid his ballet dancing son from the world press and the American electorate for months because he, or his publicity agent, thought that his offspring's lifestyle conflicted with the all-American, Marlboro cowboy image he wanted to project.

One beneficiary of divorced parents' unwillingness to come to terms over their children is the boarding schools. For those who can afford it boarding school is often regarded as one solution to the parents' problems—but not perhaps the children's. One child care specialist had this to say: 'Alternating custody and boarding school are from time to time advocated as ways of dealing with children of divorce. For the children this solves nothing. Both are attempts to please the parents. By placing a child in a boarding school he loses both parents for two-thirds of every year of his school life. At least he keeps one parent as well as continuity with his locality if he continues to live at, and go to school from one parental home.'*

Despite this, boarding school is a popular option. One headmistress commented, 'Boarding school is seen as a way to prevent one parent's influence becoming preponderant; in others, perhaps the majority, the boarding school is expected to provide stability for the child when the lives of both parents are unsettled.'**

* *The Rules of the Tug of Love Game*

** *Torn Lives* (Order of Christian Unity, 1979)

This sounds remarkably like a cop out and, if you think that is the reason why he is so keen to send little Johnny off to Winchester, you should say so.

Do not be subversive—or allow your husband to be. If their mother is a red hot communist, do not preach the delights of capitalism, or give them a copy of *The Wealth of Nations* for Christmas. Be diplomatic. Do not talk about money. And do not let your money talk about you. Keep the mink out of sight if you do have one. Do not moan about it if you don't. But be sensible. You need not go to the lengths of one second wife, resident of Knightsbridge, who would pack all her china and new clothes away when her husband's children, whose mother was remarried to a man of modest means, came to stay.

What about discipline? Unless they are disturbed, most children are only diabolically badly behaved when they are bored stiff—and that is probably as much your fault as theirs. Sometimes they may play up just to see what they can get away with. Sometimes they just get over-excited and silly. Draconian measures like a good spanking are rarely called for. When they are, leave them to your husband. That does not mean you have to stand meekly by while your sofa is shredded, your cat set alight or your clothes commandeered. Your medicine should be preventive not punitive. Diversion is the name of the game. Letting things get to the stage of retribution invites all sorts of awkward situations and invites the cry, 'You can't tell me off, because you are not my mummy.'

Do not be too impressed by protests like 'Mummy always lets us do it' when you forbid sand and water on the kitchen floor. And beware of letting them do too much of what is really forbidden at home. Their mother may resent it, thinking you are just making her job of caring for them that much more difficult.

What not to do with them is less of a problem, usually, than what to do with them. The divorced dad has become a familiar figure trailing his brood round the museums on Sunday afternoon. One minute he is living with the children and everything comes naturally. The next he is stuck in a bed-sitter wondering where to take them for the afternoon. Often it takes the children so long to settle down once they have been collected that, by the time they start behaving normally, it is time to take them home. Short afternoon meetings are not very satisfactory for anyone.

By far the best thing is to establish a relaxed situation where the children can come and stay for a couple of days, or a week's holiday. A dad is not going to keep up with his kids just taking them for an outing on Sunday afternoons. At best, he becomes a part-time entertainer and nanny. At worst, he will come to realize the hopelessness of his position and see the children less and less. Or the children may come to regard him as someone whose main function is to give mummy an afternoon off.

Many men realize on divorce how little they really know their children. Only by having them around, taking responsibility for them, doing things with and for them can they get to know them. The younger a man, the less chance there is of his being cast in the Victorian paternal mould. It is surprising how many men have never changed a nappy or given the children their tea. If the children are very young, it may be as well to find out before they come to stay how competent he is at coping with the sudden temperatures, bouts of technicolour sickness and fears of something under the bed that are the stuff of childhood. In any case, stock up on Vick, cough mixture, milk of magnesia, TCP and plenty of kneecap-sized plasters. Young children may worry about spending the night away from home—or they may see it as a big adventure. Either way, there might be a few tears. Often a little weep is solely for mum, in case she feels miserable because no one might miss her. Generally, it stops the minute she is round the corner. If you have never had children of your own, your home may be littered with fascinating bits and pieces within easy reach of a curious child. Move everything a few feet nearer the ceiling. Better still, pack it away. It saves frayed nerves when they beg you to let them play with the Royal Worcester tea set, or drink orange juice out of your best crystal. Have plenty of other things around to amuse them. Get them to bring their own toys, or to keep some permanently in their bedrooms. Be friendly towards any animals, stuffed or live—unless they want

Move everything a few feet nearer the ceiling

to bed down with mountain-sized Snoopys or a tank full of piranha fish. Do not let your husband spoil them stupid. Do not let him send them home looking like a walking tuckshop. It is bad to buy their affection (although contrary to what most people like to believe, it is often perfectly possible to do so). And nothing is more calculated to upset the most co-operative ex-wife.

How children adjust to divorce and to their parents after divorce depends on the child itself, and the way the parents behave. A very sensitive youngster, nervous and insecure even before the parents broke up, will clearly suffer more than a robust child who may accept the breakdown as a fact of life. But if the parents are fighting, things are always more difficult for the children.

Children of divorced parents are more likely to divorce themselves. The cycle of unhappiness is handed down from generation to generation. It may all be a question of example. If children see their parents bitching away at each other, they are going to have a very strange view of married life when they, in turn, come to settle down. Many ex-wives try to brainwash their children into disliking the father—and there is little he or anyone else can do about it. The golden rule is not to retaliate—at least in front of the kids.

It is, after all, rather good sport to watch your elders and supposed betters being rude about each other—rather like seeing your driving instructor caught speeding. Whatever the temptations or the provocations, never criticize their mother in front of them. It is the worst thing you can do. Nor should your husband. It might give him some short term satisfaction, but in the long term it is in the worst interests of his children.

What if the children are hostile toward you? Their attitudes may be dictated by their mother. She may stop short of running down their father but direct her attentions to you instead. Try to ignore it—and remember that very young children can be totally influenced by their mums. If she says the moon is blue, then blue it is. If she thinks that daddy's new wife is a witch, they will see broomsticks flying everywhere. Trying to turn the children against you is her way of driving a wedge between you and your husband. She is trying to make him choose between them and you. She is being irresponsible, and your husband should tell her so.

A second wife's greatest fear is that her husband's kids will object to her, and more than that—make it a reason for not wanting to visit their father. This seems to be a very common factor in squabbles over access and it is often orchestrated by an embittered ex-wife. The short answer is to make yourself scarce when they are there, thereby removing the grounds of the real or imagined (and it is usually imagined) objections. This may be a bit of a blow to your pride, but if the children's relationship with their father is really at stake, so what? Whatever you do, do not get into a situation where your husband has to choose between his kids and you. It simply is not fair.

Many second wives do get on well with their husband's children. They often establish very close relationships. The kids may even find it easier, if they are a little older, to talk to a neutral 'auntie' figure about their problems than to their real parents. Adolescents often go through a period of rejecting their mother or father, or both. In a broken family the impact can be far worse—they can simply pack their bags and go and live with daddy if they are fed up at home. Daddy may be delighted by this show of favouritism, but in reality it is just a way for the son or daughter to show their independence from their mother. It is very wrong to encourage it and, if they are still at school, it could be totally impractical. They may come and moan to you about their mother. Stop your husband telling them that great minds think alike, and point out that she is their mother, loves them, and has always done her best for them.

Later on, of course, they can choose where they live. And if they decide to move in with dad, lock, stock, barrel and record collection, it is an offer you cannot really refuse. But do not let them get the impression that life with you is a glorified holiday. Just because you have been cool, calm and collected in the short spells they have been with you, do not let them think you are not flesh and blood like ordinary mortals. Step-mothers can be one of life's great disappointments. They tend to set themselves standards so high that they cannot keep them. Or the children gain an image of perfection that may be dented by the experience of actually living with you every day. Make very sure that you know them, and they know you—warts and all—before you inflict yourselves on each other.

Oneupwomenship

DIVORCE IS EMBARRASSING. One marriage in three ends in divorce these days, but still we don't know how to handle it socially.

The science of post-marital etiquette is in its infancy, but it is vital to the second wife. How are you going to handle his friends? How will he cope with yours? There's his boss and his secretary to deal with. And the inevitable mother-in-law lying in wait for the unsuspecting second wife, full of pride and prejudices. Are you ready to handle his ex-wife? Face to face? How can you help him handle her, and the strains she will put on your marriage?

When a single girl becomes a second wife, attitudes around her change. Mostly it is because you are plunged into his world, where the ghosts of his life with wife number one linger on. You may not have changed, but your circumstances have, and you'll be reminded of it constantly.

If a man introduces an old girlfriend to his mates, that's one thing. When he introduces wife number two to those who knew wife number one, there's invariably an embarrassed pause. A second wife will worry that her husband's friends are constantly comparing her to the first. Her husband's friends, if the truth be known, are worrying about it, too. And how do you explain the situation quickly and diplomatically to new

When he introduces wife number two to those who knew wife number one, there's invariably an embarrassed pause

acquaintances? One man introduces his second wife as his 'current wife', which keeps everyone—including her—guessing. Another happily married man says, 'This is my first wife' to party guests, who spend the rest of the evening searching feverishly for the non-existent number two. It is a ripe area for comedy, but too many people are nonplussed by it all. To add to the confusion divorced wives keep their husbands' names. There is no recognized way of denoting that this is the former Mrs Smith. The family courts, indeed, have the rather unsettling habit of calling the divorced pair 'the husband' and 'the wife' years after the marriage has been dissolved and they have both remarried. One second wife was shocked to hear a judge talk to her husband about 'your wife'—referring to his ex-wife—during a legal squabble.

Hostesses find divorce and remarriage highly inconvenient. Do they invite both, just one or neither? And what do they do about the new wives or husbands? Most friends and acquaintances find it very difficult to adjust to different domestic arrangements or, through embarrassment or sympathy (some would say prejudice) for one side, are unwilling to try.

The rich have been able to afford divorce for longer than the rest of us, so they are more practised at living with it. Wealth can oil the wheels in the stickiest situation. When Mrs Money II meets Mrs Money I she can afford to be far more civilized—on the surface at least—than her semi-detached equivalent. How, after all, can you have a decent row about being abandoned in a mansion in Hampstead with several gold bars to your name?

There are fewer of the rich *and* famous and they tend to have more wives per head. The law of averages dictates that they meet more frequently. A theatrical agent, quizzed by one expectant gossip columnist if Bruce Forsyth and Anthea Redfern would appear professionally together after separation observed that if ex-wives and husbands refused to work with each other, most stars would never tread the boards again.

Was it sheer chance, or foresight on Allah's part, that the hyper-wealthy Arabs are polygamous?

If the rich manage their wives in a civilized way, the extremely rich have an even better system. Was it sheer chance, or foresight on Allah's part that the hyper-wealthy Arabs are polygamous? Being married to all of your wives all of the time may be less of a problem than being married to all of them one at a time.

Further down the social scale, things are not so relaxed. A second wife can be an embarrassment to everyone. An acquaintance your husband hasn't seen in years tells you enthusiastically that you haven't changed a bit since last you met. And he can remember what you were wearing, drinking and saying with unerring accuracy. Trouble is, it's not you he is flattering—it's her.

Your husband's closest friends are the worst hurdle. Their loyalties are not so much divided as torn apart and borne off as trophies of war. Divorcing couples find they cannot share out friends like furniture, the china or the coffee set. However amicable a divorce, however enlightened and jolly it is, their friends usually find it impossible to stand by both of them in their new lives. They invariably end up with both feet in one camp.

One solicitor told how he and his wife had been great friends with another young married couple for years. They lived on the same estate, did the same sorts of things and saw a lot of each other. The couple came to a parting of the ways. It was an amicable divorce. So much so that they wanted the solicitor to act for both of them—something he could not do. But after the divorce the solicitor and his wife found visits and contact becoming less and less frequent. When both of the divorced couple remarried, the new partners would come and visit with them. But things were never the same. The friendships all but evaporated. There was no taking sides or bad feeling. The remarriages, if anything, made keeping up more difficult.

Alone after the break up, the divorced usually elicit a bit of sympathy and comfort. Once they have found pastures new, people feel less concerned about them. Even those who managed reasonably civilized divorces say how damaging it is to their social life. Friends just do not seem able to cope with it. Sometimes they may only have liked one of the couple anyway. Divorce is a great way of finding out who your friends weren't. A husband will have more in common with people at work. His wife is probably welcome to her monopoly of the neighbours. She may be delighted, moreover, to see the back of the darts team for good. He may be vastly relieved that he no longer has to be nice to his wife's best friend's husband,

Divorce is a great way of finding out who your friends weren't

who smokes incessantly, has smelly feet or interminably discusses the way to cut five minutes off his journey home.

Some couples make a good double act, but can be dreadfully dreary without the other half. Watching them peck away at each other may have provided hours of innocent entertainment over the years, and livened up boring dinner parties no end. But apart they might be less compulsive viewing.

If the divorce was a messy affair, your husband's friends will probably be too weary to want to know you, him or even her any more. Friends are the luckless bystanders caught up in the suburban guerrilla war between divorcing couples. Everything is propaganda. Friends find their talent for diplomacy tested to the limit if they try to play fair with both sides. For each side, the price of continuing friendship is opposition to the other. It makes for a pretty high mortality rate among friends. But what about those who survive?

Friends who knew your husband and his first wife as a couple may not necessarily be hostile—but they can be difficult to deal with. They are probably more embarrassed by the past than you. When old friends get together, they talk about things they have done, seen, eaten or drunk together. Among those who have been married for a time, the great debates are over which school little Mark is going to, where to stock up the freezer, what new car to buy. They are all too aware that every turn in the conversation may lead to she who should not be mentioned. Talk may become so small as to be virtually non-existent. It ruins spontaneity if everyone is desperately worried about dropping a clanger. It can be worse than downright hostility. At least then you know your toes are going to be trodden on. It is hardly surprising that many friendships which survive divorce are killed off by remarriage.

However a second wife needn't be a social outcast. Study your social survival kit and you will find you can still win over his friends and influence people.

Don't make a fuss, pull a face, stamp your foot or make rude comments when friends mention his ex-wife. If someone should apologize for mentioning her name, see it as a good opportunity to show how little it worries you. After all, you wouldn't expect your husband to get upset and jealous every time someone mentioned your old flame.

There *is* life before remarriage. It is silly to be hypersensitive about his ex. Some husbands try to behave as though wife

Don't make a fuss, pull a face, stamp your foot or make rude comments when friends mention his ex-wife

number one never existed. But you shouldn't expect him or his friends to rewrite history—or to discuss his divorce in hushed tones like some family mishap in a period romance. You should, in fact, make a positive effort to put everyone at their ease. If they like your husband, his friends will probably want to like you as well. It is so much more convenient that way. The act of supreme confidence and oneupwomanship is to say something nice about his ex—or, even better—repeat something nice your husband has said about her. If neither of you can think of anything, make something up.

This will make it plain that your husband's friends are free to mention her name without risk of sending you into a tantrum or deep depression. If Daphne du Maurier's faint-hearted heroine could manage it, anyone can. 'Of course she was so clever,' warbled the bishop's wife in *Rebecca* to literature's most feeble-minded second wife. 'She stopped, turning a little pink, fearing loss of tact. But I agreed with her at once to save embarrassment, and I heard myself saying boldly, brazenly, "Rebecca must have been a wonderful person." I could not believe that I had said the name at last. I waited, wondering what would happen. I had said the name. I had said the word Rebecca aloud. It was a tremendous relief. It was as though I had taken a purge and rid myself of an intolerable pain.' With luck, you will find the experience less melodramatic. But it can be difficult all the same.

If you know his ex-wife is pumping out subversive propaganda you may feel you are casting your pearls before swine. It may be tempting to try to get your own back. Swallow hard and tell yourself everyone will admire your self-restraint. More important you will not put his friends, who may still be seeing his ex-wife, in the unhappy position of having to choose between her and you. Anything you say may be taken back and used in evidence against you. It may seem fun to return abuse through a third party, but it's not too bright. Far better not to give her the satisfaction of knowing that she is upsetting you. If one of his friends draws you aside and rants on about how he loathed your husband's first wife and how pleased he is that he has found a nice girl like you do not rise or, more appropriately, sink, to the bait. Never let a nasty word about her pass your lips in public. Curse her in private if you must.

Some of his friends might feel that aggression is the better part of valour. Wives tend to sympathize with wives, and wives make the social arrangements. More women than men initiate divorce proceedings, but we are stuck with the stereotypes of the poor abandoned wife and the 'other woman'. His friends might blame you for the break-up. They may sympathize with his ex who regards you as the root of all evil. Perhaps she has been getting at her ex-husband through getting at you. Wives of well known philanderers have found it cheaper and infinitely more gratifying to hound their husbands through the gossip columns than send them solicitors' letters. Once upon a time well bred wives were expected to take their husbands' misdemeanour lying down. But trying to shame your errant spouse into returning home by plastering your troubles all over the newspapers has become quite fashionable. The prize must go to Vivien Merchant, the Shakespearian actress. She remarked to the press when her husband Harold Pinter had left her for Lady Antonia Fraser that it didn't matter that he had left all his shoes at home: Lady Antonia's feet were so big, she remarked tartly, he could probably wear hers. Runner-up must be Bruce Forsyth's first wife. Asked about his marriage to Anthea Redfern, a glamorous blonde some twenty years her junior, she said vaguely that yes, she must have met her some time, but she simply couldn't remember her.

Lesser mortals have to make do with their friends and acquaintances for an audience. And ex-wives frequently go to town on the propaganda. They may not want to be beastly to your husband, but merely demonstrate solidarity with his ex. Once it is clear you are not the scheming heartless siren your husband's ex-wife makes you out to be, his friends may accept and like you on your own terms. Or they may not. Even after a glimpse of your beauty, charm and accomplishments they may still be hostile, on principle. There is not much you can do to overcome such ideological differences. Just try not to take it personally. Do not discourage your husband's friendship with such numbskulls. You might feel a little hurt about it. But let him meet them if he wants on his own, without a torrent of recrimination when he returns.

Why do so many married couples feel they have to do everything together? Why do they feel that they should share all their friends—that there is something wrong or strange about one partner keeping up acquaintances the other doesn't like, find interesting, or approve of? In second marriage there is far more scope for such differences of opinion. The age gap between husband and wife is usually greater than in a first marriage—particularly where the man has been divorced and the second wife was single.

Traditionally wives have been younger than their husbands. Second wives are much younger. More than half of them are over four years junior whereas only a quarter of first wives were that much younger. While only two in a hundred first wives are ten years or more younger than their husbands, a quarter of the second wives are a decade apart. The same rules apply to remarried ex-wives. First time around, eight out of ten husbands are older than the wives. But around half of the men who marry divorced women are younger than their partners. The cult of the older woman seems less a tribute to the powers of ginseng and jogging than the rush of divorced women hunting a mate.

You might expect a second marriage to be more tolerant. But that is not necessarily so. One second wife who had floated on the edges of the jet set before marrying a divorced man nearly ten years older would not dare talk about her old life while he was in the room. He became terribly upset if she mentioned her old friends and acquaintances of whom he clearly did not approve.

Because of a difference in age you may find your husband and your friends are poles apart. He may be well established in a career—they may still be thinking about it. They may think his tastes verge on the geriatric. He may find them immature. If your contemporaries are mainly single they may find his preoccupation with ex-wives and children strange. You yourself may think his friends come from another planet. There may be no common point of interest between your friends and his, apart from you. Is there really much to be gained by dragging him to your friend's bottle party, or his taking you to the Tory club social? Couples who compromise by doing neither end up going nowhere, except to the divorce court.

Make sure you hang on to your friends. If your husband has children by his first marriage, he will be trotting off to visit them. He might want to help out if there is a panic over homework or some domestic mishap. He may want to take them and his ex-wife out on occasions like a birthday. You'll feel less resentful of these calls on his time (not to mention his money) if you, too, have some life of your own. It is difficult to feel left out when you are whooping it up with friends while he's submerged beneath milk shakes and chips at McDonald's. And he'll not be stricken with guilt—just indigestion.

One woman in his life you cannot afford to ignore is his secretary

One woman in his life you cannot afford to ignore is his secretary. Make friends with her. She's the one who keeps wives apart, and her boss together. Put up with her faintly proprietorial air—she may have known your husband for longer than you have. If you want to go down well with his business colleagues she is the one to butter up. She has the time, curiosity and inclination to find out about you and broadcast her views.

Make sure you are on Christian name terms. That way when you telephone him at the office you will avoid the most crushing encounter of all. 'And which Mrs Smith would that be, dear?'

His mother, though, is the real challenge. Compared to her, dealing with his friends and acquaintances is a piece of cake. Divorce gives her the biggest opportunity to organize, or disorganize, her offspring's life since she demanded he cut his hair, stopped smoking or turned the record player down twenty years before.

Whether she loved or loathed his ex, whether she mourns or rejoices in the death of the marriage is incidental. Deep down in her heart, she knows that wives may come and wives may go, but mum stays on for ever. Friends may be tactful and discreet to the point of speechlessness, but mothers-in-law rarely suffer such inhibitions. They are supposed to be bad enough first time around. Second time around, they can become impossible. It may be all very well for a son to tell his mother not to interfere, but if he has clearly made a mess of his first marriage, it is harder for him to demand that she should keep her nose out of his second. At the very least, he may feel in her debt because she stood by him in the break-up.

Naturally many mothers-in-law are not kindly disposed towards their sons' ex-wives. But they may still chat on about them in an embarrassing fashion all the same. One second wife said, 'His mother hated Sandy (the ex-wife). But at lunch last Sunday she just kept going on and on about her. Sandy said this, Sandy did that. In the end Paul's brother suggested that it really wasn't very polite of her to talk about Sandy in front of me.'

It is comforting to think that whatever she may think of you she will be thinking worse of your predecessor. But second wives often feel that their husbands' families do not really take them seriously. One second wife, herself divorced and remarried, said that it was only when she started producing babies that her new husband's parents, who had no grandchildren to date, really started treating her as a member of the family. Till then they had been distinctly cool. For the sake of your husband you may be anxious to please his mother—but do not let her trample all over you.

. . . please his mother—but do not let her trample all over you

She may have disapproved violently of his ex from the very beginning. And never forget it is supreme oneupwomanship to show she has been proved right: her opinions on everything are thereby elevated to the wisdom of a Delphic Oracle—in her eyes, at least. You may think you have found an ally. But just because she's against the opposition doesn't mean she is on your side—or even that she's fighting the same war. If she rattles on about how her former daughter-in-law failed to keep the house, garden, children and her husband—be warned. Her criticism is an implied threat, not a compliment to you. You are not likely to please this sort of mother-in-law, however hard you try. She will probably be opposed to you on principle whether you keep the house like a surgical ward or a bomb site.

On the other hand, she might think his ex was wonderful. It

is really just the other side of the same interfering coin. She is really more concerned with what suits her than what suits her son. Never crawl around with the ego of a snail, imagining his ex-wife was a mixture of Wonderwoman and a detergent advertisement mum.

Even if his mother is well intentioned, she might find it impossible to resist making comparisons between you and your predecessor. You cannot lap up her praise one minute, and mope about the brickbats the next. It is a friendly form of blackmail. The secret is not to care. Once she senses you are pleased or worried that you do this or that better or worse than the ex, she's won. Refuse to compete with your husband's ex-wife by proxy. And start off as you mean to continue. Don't set your standards higher than usual in order to impress her and then work yourself into a frenzy trying to keep up the pretence—or even worse, let your good intentions dramatically lapse overnight, under the usual mountain of washing-up.

It is quite usual for the first wife to keep in touch with her former mother-in-law after divorce—particularly if there are children. Grandparents dread that the kids will be whipped away after divorce, and they will never see them again. Since the wife usually calls the tune on this, the husband's parents have the most to lose. They have to remain friendly with your husband's ex-wife, like her or not. And it can be a very good thing. It is certainly no slight to you. Grandparents can act as an effective buffer between two hostile parties. But they should be trained to keep their mouths shut about you and your husband's private lives. If you win the pools or your tycoon uncle suddenly pops off, you do not want his ex to be the second person to know. Similarly, you shouldn't expect your mother-in-law to break faith with her. Indiscretions rarely work one way. You cannot complain if she drops a clanger with the ex, when you have pumped her for information the day before.

What about your husband's first wife? However hard you try and forget about his first marriage, you will probably be dying of curiosity and suffering terminal jealousy. If he divorced her to marry you, you might just have the odd twinge of guilt as well. If he's got kids, his relationship with his ex may splutter on for years. Ex-wives sometimes exploit the situation. Second wives resent it. The poor chap in the middle makes up his mind to become a monk next time around.

Some second wives get on well with their predecessors. Even when, moreover, ex-wife and husband can hardly say 'good morning' to each other without having an argument about it. One husband found that all messages and instructions about the children were funnelled through the second wife, who used to keep the peace by listening patiently while the ex-wife poured forth her catalogue of woes. Despite feeling furious about her ex-husband she never vented her anger on the second wife, who doubled as a psychiatrist's couch for her predecessor. But such a relationship is rare. Logically a second wife should be able to tolerate a first wife. In the same way that she might enjoy hearing about or seeing some other place or person from her husband's past. He loved her once, he loves you now so presumably there is some sort of link. What usually happens is that you have hardly a good word to say about each other. Not because you are intrinsically incompatible but because most such relationships hinge on his attitude to her, her attitude to him, and consequently, you.

A real drama or crisis can bring wives together. One ex-wife who collapsed under the nervous strain of her divorce became friends with her successor when they all had to live together under one roof with the children while she recovered. Asked by a television interviewer what she felt about the second wife she said, yes she liked her a lot. But she couldn't resist saying that she felt a bit sorry for her, being lumbered with her ex-husband. Benign indifference is probably the best you can hope for. If his ex-wife has a matter of fact approach to the divorce, there should be few problems. If there were no children, there should be no reason why you should cross paths, let alone swords, with her at all. But if there is any reason for further communication—money or children, for instance, life becomes more difficult.

People talk piously about having a 'good divorce'. Leo Abse, the Member of Parliament who was one of the sponsors of the 1969 Divorce Reform Act, has often said that healthy divorce is as important as healthy marriage. Very few couples manage to have anything other than a very unhealthy one. A good divorce requires the patience of a saint allied to the diplomatic flair of Metternich, particularly under the present law: the kind of qualities, in fact, that would avoid the problem in the first place.

How you cope with his ex-wife really depends on her attitude to you. The arrival of a second wife on the scene can alter the attitude of the first towards her divorce or her ex-husband. She can accept his philanderings through the years as evidence of immaturity. However many girlfriends and affairs he may have notched, she may console herself that she is the only wife. She can say her marriage collapsed because he was just not good husband material. Any signs of wanting to marry someone else comes as a blow to her self-esteem—even though she may want a divorce anyway.

Sometimes it is only when their ex-husbands remarry . . .

Sometimes it is only when their ex-husbands remarry that first wives start agitating about the maintenance. One ex-wife, who had been divorced four years earlier and received no maintenance, suddenly pleaded that she was too ill to work and claimed—and got—a third of the husband's income. The wife of a wealthy banker was perfectly happy with the five star arrangements made for their divorce until she discovered, through a friend, that her husband's girlfriend was expecting a baby and he was desperate to marry her. The price of her co-operation virtually doubled overnight.

Husbands often think that there is a great deal to be said for wives being kept firmly apart. First wives and second wives provoke each other. She resents seeing you with him. Your blood boils at the money he pays her.

If his ex is cool, calm and collected about the whole thing, how friendly should you become? She may have remarried and no longer have an axe to grind. She may be delighted with her divorce. Should you invite her to your home? Should you go to her place? At Christmas should you all get together with the kids?

However troubled their parents' marriage was, children ache to have them back together again. Watching them and their new partners being super-cool and reasonable about the whole thing can make it even harder for the kids. At a recent headmasters' conference one speaker told of a pupil whose parents had divorced and married new partners. The child was so confused by the appearance together of all four parents and step-parents at school open day that he was found sobbing his heart out on the playing field while they were all chortling merrily together. While it is clearly bad for children to see parents at each other's throats, it may be equally traumatic to see them behaving as though the divorce had never happened.

Chumminess between ex-husbands and wives doesn't do much for second wives' confidence either. Some ex-wives are deliberately gushing to their successors as a way of patronizing them. They make out they are sorry for you, being lumbered with one of their cast-offs. Husbands hate this sort of thing, and no wonder. You should really try to steer a middle course, standing your ground, but at a distance.

However you have to accept the fact he might have to see her, phone her, discuss the children and money with her. Many second wives loathe this. Either they imagine their predecessor is some Mata Hari plotting to lure him away, or they get cross because she treats him badly and he may have no option but to put up with it. Whether she is ghastly or gorgeous to him, it is probably equally unpalatable to you. Indeed if she is nice to him you might feel worse about it. If she is in the business of extracting more money, for instance, it costs you as much if she does it with a smile or a grimace. If you find it irritates or upsets you it is better that you do not know the details. A second wife should have a handy list of excuses to leave the room when her husband's ex phones.

Money – His? Hers? Yours?

MONEY BRINGS MANY of the nastiest headaches after divorce, and breaks up more second marriages than anything else. If he found life with one wife expensive, with two it can be crippling. The law leans over backwards to favour the first wife. Unless she is very careful, the second wife will find it is not just herself she is giving away in marriage, but a tidy part of her pay packet.

His money is mainly hers, as you'll soon discover. It takes a divorce to show you what the marriage vows are all about. 'With all my worldly goods I thee endow' is a promise honoured to the letter only when things turn sour. It's far more relevant to a divorce than a marriage contract. Like that anachronistic pledge of wifely obedience it should be dropped from the sacrament—or at least made an optional extra. Married, a wife has no specific claim on the housekeeping. She cannot demand a fixed portion of her husband's salary, or get his employers to give her part of his wage packet each week. Divorced she takes command of the purse-strings. And it's first come, first served.

What is an ex-wife entitled to? Very little, according to her husband. Around one third of the joint income, say the courts. More or less everything, she will say. If she doesn't work or remarry and has a couple of children, your average semi-detached husband can reckon on saying good-bye to around half of his annual salary. How can he possibly afford to marry *you?* How can he afford *not* to marry you? When he gets on his knees and says he just can't live without you, at least you know he's being utterly sincere.

Many divorced men simply cannot contemplate remarriage because of the financial burden of divorce. The relaxation of the divorce laws a decade ago created the appetite for remarriage but destroyed the capacity. As Mr Micawber might have said if he were alive and divorced today—one wife, one income may equal unhappiness, but two wives, one income could mean misery.

Getting your husband's first mistake married off again is a top priority

What he has to pay depends on his, her and even your circumstances. Theoretically it works both ways. If his ex was a female tycoon or an heiress she might end up paying him, providing he does not actually *marry* you. It would be nice if you could choose your husband's ex-wife for him. Best would be a full blown career woman who earned far more than her ex-husband. Rich women have been known to pay off their husbands handsomely. Christina Onassis is rumoured to have given her third spouse a couple of tankers so he could paddle his own canoe. But, alas, even Barbara Hutton's cast-offs are limited in number and such prizes still thin on the ground in this liberated age.

Next best is an ex who is likely to get married again. Once she is hitched, or rather rehitched, the dire financial responsibility is offloaded on to her new husband. Should this hapless being run away or fall under a bus the day after the wedding it is her, not to mention his, bad luck. She cannot come back to husband number one for maintenance for herself again. Getting your husband's first mistake married off again is top priority. It is far more important than your own wedding.

The younger she is the better her chances. More than half the people who get divorced marry again within five years. After the age of fifty, women's chances of remarriage wither somewhat. But the younger their children are, the more likely they are to remarry. Particularly reassuring is the number of bachelors marrying older divorced women.

If he was foolish enough to marry someone no one wants to run off with, life could become very expensive. An annual salary can only go so far—usually as far as a first wife. Take a man on £10,000 a year. He might be expected to cough up over £3,000 in maintenance for her, plus up to £1,000 each for a couple of children. And he might be paying part of the mortgage and school fees, too.

But what about Women's Lib? What about it indeed! We are constantly told we live in the age of the emancipated woman, the era of equal opportunity when the working wife

. . . since the first ape man gave the second ape man a bunch of bananas in return for marrying his daughter

and mother is the norm, not the exception. Why then, you may ask, is your husband forced to pay vast sums of money to keep his ex-wife in wall-to-wall idleness? He is doing what most men have done since the first ape man gave the second ape man a bunch of bananas in return for marrying his daughter. This simple act set the pace, not to mention the place for women ever since. All through history we have been regarded as goods and chattels and a financial liability. Our fathers couldn't even give us away. Our prospective husbands had to be bribed with dowries, sheep or oxen, or even whole countries, before they could be persuaded to marry us.

Despite the changes in society, the concept has scarcely altered. Man is still regarded as the provider, not only when he is married but after he is divorced as well. Wives—particularly ex-wives—are still regarded as weaker vessels into which never-ending income must be poured. The financial aftermath of divorce makes a mockery of the concept of the 'clean break'—it is more like a very messy divide across which both sides continue to hurl abuse long after the marriage is legally dead and buried. While no one disputes the obligation of a father to provide for his children, there is growing doubt about the justice of letting an ex-wife live off her husband for the rest of her life. Despite legally enforced equality of opportunity, and that a third of the country's workforce are women, half of them married, Britain clings to archaic family laws.

Britain is now the exception rather than the rule. Many other countries have abandoned the notion of lifelong maintenance. Australia, Germany, Canada and Sweden treat the man and woman as equal partners in divorce. Once a woman's children are at school, or grown up, she cannot expect to be supported by her former husband for good.

If, philosophically, everything about maintenance is at odds with the accepted status of women then, practically, it is completely out of place where there is easy, quick 'no fault' divorce and a third of the population looks like having at least two marriages by the end of the century.

The overriding principle, laid down in the Matrimonial Causes Act 1973, says that post-divorce financial settlements 'should place the parties, so far as is practicable, and, having regard to their conduct, just to do so, in the financial position in which they would have been if the marriage had not broken down'. This is clearly pie in the sky for all except the very rich. For ordinary mortals it is clearly impossible to keep two people separately for the price of one. It leaves those at the middle and lower levels of the income scale with the right to remarry but without the means.

Among the lawyers and theoreticians there are two schools of thought. One view is that all maintenance for ex-wives (though not for children) should be abolished. Maintenance should be paid only when there are very young children involved or for a limited period when an ex-wife is looking or training for a job. The opposing view is that it is all very well to talk about the equality of women and claim that they can work for a living—but the fact of the matter is that time at home rearing children means lost career opportunities and, therefore, less pay. So, the ex-wife should be compensated.

However, many divorced women break up their homes against the wishes of their husbands. And there is many a bewildered and financially battered husband left wondering how and why he has lost his children, his wife, his home and a large portion of his income forever through no particular fault of his own. In the old days things were a little different. If a woman ran off with the milkman and was divorced for adultery, she would not expect maintenance. If, on the other hand, her husband eloped with his secretary and his wife divorced him, she would, as the innocent party, receive maintenance. The 1969 Act abolished the idea of a 'guilty' party. When it comes to fixing the financial provisions, conduct is usually ignored. Lord Denning in a famous Court of Appeal decision said it was only to be taken into account if it was 'gross and obvious'.* That, like everything else in divorce, is subject to individual interpretation. A wife who goes off with her husband's best friend would probably find that it made not one iota of difference to the financial settlement. That is what most people find hardest

* Wachtel v. Wachtel, 1973

to understand—why on earth should a man be forced to pay for the pleasure of being deserted? The answer is that we have more or less done away with the idea of the matrimonial offence. It appears only as evidence of the breakdown of a marriage, not as the grounds for ending it. So a wandering wife who brings the dissolution of her marriage on herself will find her claim to a share of her husband's income intact. It will probably make no difference whether she slept with the whole of her husband's football team or was a real little shrinking violet. Whether he was Sir Galahad or Attila the Hun, her husband will probably end up paying through the nose.

The present laws were supposed to do away with those long juicy divorce cases that provided the Sunday newspapers with so many stories and the private detective with so much employment. 'Guilt' was supposed to be a thing of the past. The trouble is that, when one party is paying money and the other receiving it, it feels to the husband that he is being punished. And not only the husband. A second wife will find that an ex-wife who has not conveniently died or remarried will take priority over her when it comes to sharing out the income. One woman's maintenance is often another woman's pay packet.

Even if a second wife has no intention of giving up work after remarriage it is still galling to think she *must* work in order to provide his first wife with privileges that she hasn't even had the opportunity to reject in the first place. The trouble is that unless an ex-wife is a high-flyer, there may be little incentive for her to work. Not all ex-wives, of course, are content to live off their ex-husbands. But the way is clear for those who want, through greed, vengeance, or plain idleness, to do so.

The law bends in the favour of a divorced wife in a way that makes the leaning tower of Pisa look positively upright. The angle of the incline depends, among other things, on where you live. In some parts there are registrars who might mistake the name Germaine Greer for a new strain of measles, so out of touch do they seem with reality. Research by the Centre for Socio-Legal Studies at Wolfson College, Oxford, showed how old fashioned is the thinking of some of the registrars who make, or amend, the bulk of maintenance orders.

Asked what they would do in the case of a young childless wife divorcing after a short marriage, 19% of the registrars said they would grant her a full order. Only 11% thought that she could start earning her own living immediately without any maintenance at all. Over half would have granted a small or nominal order—which means that for as long as she has not remarried a divorced wife can come back time and time again for more. The registrars seemed divided on basic questions like whether ex-wives should be expected to work or be kept by their former husbands. Whether a man gets stuck with a liberal or a reactionary can make a huge difference to his bank account. One registrar said, 'Where the wife has never worked I would always take it into account, but divorce could not give a bread ticket for life and I would always expect a young woman to do something to earn her living.' Another said, 'If she had no job and the husband says it is easy for her to go out and get money I would say, "Did you marry her with a view to her going out to work to supplement the family income?" And, if not, she would get an order ... even if only 25 or 30 she would get an order.'

The law is so vague, or so flexible, that the registrars have enormous discretion. But one man's discretion is another's inconsistency. They make bizarre decisions that would offend anyone's sense of justice. A young policeman and his wife, who had no children, divorced after a short marriage. The wife got a nominal maintenance order of £1 a week. After her divorce she lived with a boyfriend by whom she had a baby. She went back to the court saying she could not work because of the baby, and succeeded in getting a maintenance order of £10 a week from her former husband. The Court of Appeal eventually reduced the amount to £3. Even so it insisted on upholding the ridiculous notion that her former husband was still in some way responsible for her.*

Once she has been granted an order, however small, a

* Wagner v. Wagner, 1978

divorced first wife will forever have more legal right to your husband's money than you have. It gives her a permanent stake in his future.

It does not work the other way round. It is rare to find a mother who has abandoned her children paying maintenance to the father. But a divorced man who is unemployed, for instance, may be expected to keep up part or all of his maintenance obligations. Husbands who are out of work can rarely expect anything from their comfortably employed wives. Indeed one professional man who lost his job, far from being able to claim maintenance from his wife, found a nominal maintenance order made against him, just in case he found work in the future.* The courts are still ludicrously reluctant to recognize that an ex-wife is entirely responsible for herself. Indeed the ex-wife who says she doesn't want a nominal order often surprises the court.

While a former husband's responsibility to his ex-wife seems never ending, the courts are only too happy to ignore his obligations to the second. The courts' general attitude is that second wives knew what they were letting themselves in for when they were married. If only it were true.

Most macabre of all is the former wife of a marriage that ended years ago who comes out of the blue to claim her pound—or indeed several thousands of pounds—of flesh. Her husband may never have paid her maintenance—because at the time of the divorce she was working—and there were no children to support. To all intents and purposes it was a clean break. But even in those circumstances it is likely that her solicitor would have obtained a nominal order—say £1 a year, and the husband would have thought no more about it. Years later the ex-wife may lose her job, fall ill, or just wake up to the fact that the trainee chartered accountant she divorced is now the boss of International Widgets. She can revive the maintenance order and obtain substantial sums from her ex-husband.

He may have a new wife (he may have worked his way through several), a family, and be mortgaged up to the hilt. No

* Bennett v. Bennett, Court of Appeal, 1978

matter, the court would probably recognize the first wife's claim.

One second wife, who works as a truck driver, married a divorced man who had custody of the children of his first marriage. She had a child from her first marriage. The ex-wife took money in settlement of her divorce, and the husband paid no maintenance because she was working and he had the children. Two years later his ex-wife claimed she could no longer work because of an illness. She took her ex-husband to court and won a third of his very modest salary. When the second wife wanted to protest because her family was being clobbered, she was told that it was none of her business. But quite clearly she herself was working, not just to support her child, but to support the children of the ex-wife as well, and to help her husband pay his former wife's maintenance.

Only if a first wife has remarried or agreed to have a lump sum in lieu of maintenance or a fixed term maintenance is an ex-husband safe.

Perhaps most irritating of all the abuses of the present divorce law is where an ex-wife adopts a 'live in'—or rather a 'live off'—boyfriend. Gradually it emerges she has no intention of getting married—why should she while she is enjoying two incomes instead of one? Delight that your husband may soon be off the financial hook forever may turn to dismay when it becomes clear he is supporting two for the price of one. Proving that she is being supported by the lodger is very difficult. And a court may take no notice of it anyway. Divorcees seem to have a fatal fascination (fatal for their husbands) for wandering minstrels, jobbing builders and others whose attachments to a fixed abode or a regular wage are tenuous to say the least. They can skip the nest a few days before a court hearing, returning afterwards. An ex-husband may have to go through this circus several times at vast expense in legal fees before he gets anywhere. And there is always the possibility that Lothario, faced with the prospect of a substantial cut in his income will pack it in altogether.

Most ex-wives want to remarry—particularly if their former hubby has found a new bride. There is an enormous *me too* feeling among divorcees. A lot of them never stop to consider whether they will be better off married or just living with someone. But if, as maintenance payments roll on, patience runs out, and there is no sign of any desire to get down to marriage lines, there are some useful ploys. Your husband could, in the nicest possible way, manipulate her into marriage.

'Why doesn't he want to marry you then?'

'Well it hardly makes sense with the amount of money you are paying me, does it?'

'Ah, that's his excuse is it? Heard that one before.'

This kind of chat puts the onus on her to prove her husband wrong. The only way she can do that is to remarry. Never underestimate the oneupwomanship in divorce. Even when it is amicable, the desire to be seen doing better than the former partner frequently overrides rational behaviour.

But if she has not remarried, an ex-wife can keep going back to court every year to claim a chunk of her husband's pay rise. She does not have to prove she is starving in order to get it. If she was used to living in a luxury home, having two cars to drive, and buying the groceries at Harrods, a registrar might well agree with her that a semi in Penge, a mini and a budget account at Tesco is not good enough.

Worse, anyone in a steady job can have an attachment of earnings order made against him. This means that his employers send to the court the ex-wife's maintenance before they pay him. It is all rather undignified. We have abolished jail as a penalty for debtors, but not for failing to keep up maintenance payments. Two thousand men a year are actually sentenced to jail. Unless you want him languishing at Her Majesty's pleasure, covered in little arrows, he had better pay up.

There are alternatives. If your husband is fairly well heeled, or if his share in his home is worth a great deal, he might feel he could pay off his ex-wife with a lump sum, instead of never-ending maintenance (he would still, of course, have to pay maintenance for the children). It can take a lot of money but, if the lawyers tie it up properly, this can be the end of the matter. It may seem expensive at the time but, if the ex never remarries, you and your husband may have got the best of the bargain in the end.

If she remarries shortly afterwards, you will have both lost out. Sorting out the financial arrangements in divorce is a game of bluff and double bluff. A husband can be compelled to reveal his financial details in court. But a wife is not necessarily asked if she has plans to marry again. She may have the champagne on ice, the wedding bells may be ringing. But she can go into court and receive oodles of cash in lieu of maintenance with no obligation to mention that she is just waiting to get to the register office on time.

One solicitor had a client who, completely unknown to her estranged husband, was planning to remarry as soon as the divorce was through. She demanded, and got, a £20,000 lump sum settlement in lieu of maintenance from the husband, and remarried a fortnight after the decree absolute. The solicitor, at least, was gentleman enough to own up to a few sleepless nights over that one.

One of the most galling aspects of it all is the enormous interest shown by the ex-wife and her solicitors in your finances. It is only when the second wife is earning money that the courts take any interest in her at all. It seems particularly harsh that they will then pounce on her earnings, or even her earning capacity, in order to push up the amount a husband is forced to pay his ex-wife.

Never tell your husband how much you earn. If you have inherited anything do not be too precise about the details. The Inland Revenue will now allow a wife to fill in her own tax return form so there is no more reason for him to know your financial details than for you to know his. In the circumstances, there may be even less reason. If he doesn't know how much you earn he cannot tell a lie and he cannot tell the truth.

If there is a barney about money, you may get a letter from his ex-wife's solicitors asking for details of your pay and assets.

Never tell your husband how much you earn

Ignore it. Such requests usually come from nosey ex-wives who want to stir things up, or stock up on ammunition for the next onslaught on your husband. Second wives often fall for it, thinking they are legally obliged to tell all. One second wife, whose husband was fighting a swingeing claim from his ex was asked to give her financial details. The ex-wife's solicitors sifted through cheque stubs and Barclaycard receipts to their hearts' content. They queried birthday presents she had bought her husband, and went through everything with a fine tooth comb. Some time later she discovered it was all unnecessary.

The court can order a husband's affairs to be revealed, but not those of his second wife, who is not a party to the proceedings.* Her husband may be asked how much she earns. One trick is for the ex-wife to make such extravagant claims about her successor's wealth that the only way to prevent a court thinking the second wife is heiress to at least ten fortunes is to give them the truth. The wording of the law is very vague—the courts are supposed to consider all the circumstances. How

* But see Wilkinson v. Wilkinson, Court of Appeal, 1979, where the ex-wife successfully appealed against a registrar's refusal to direct the second wife to file an affidavit of means.

they square this with their habit of ignoring a second wife is a mystery. But a second wife's income will certainly be considered one of the circumstances, while a second wife's needs will probably not.

In fact the courts should not be concerned whether you are a managing director on £16,000 a year, or a shorthand typist on £5,000. It is not their business to query your extravagance in buying underwear from Janet Reger rather than Woolworth. What they should be interested in is whether you are self-supporting, or if you can contribute to the family budget. (A mortgage shared is a mortgage halved.)

But courts are going beyond this. One man earning £6,000 a year paid his ex-wife £5,000 because his second wife was earning £6,000. Another case established for the first time that a second wife might be ordered by the court to file an affidavit of means. This is what the divorced husband has to do when his ex-wife takes him to court for maintenance. The court said a first wife did not have to show that the second wife's wealth or income was actually being shared with her husband before it became relevant to her case for more maintenance. In another case a husband appealed against a maintenance order which gave over a third of his income to his ex-wife and the transfer of a property worth £48,000 completely to her. In dismissing his appeal the judge commented that the husband's gross income, adding in that of his mistress, was £14,000 a year.

One second wife, years before her husband's divorce, let alone his remarriage, had inherited a few thousand pounds. One day, out of the blue, the husband received a maintenance demand from his ex-wife, who had been working since the divorce but now claimed that she couldn't because she had a bad arm. There were no children of the marriage, which had only lasted a few years. The second wife ended up having to go to court. The ex-wife's solicitors had been to her mother's grave in order to trace the will at Somerset House. A copy was attached to the ex-wife's affidavit, of which two-thirds was a discussion about the second wife's supposed riches. The affidavit also suggested that the second wife, who worked part time because she had a schoolboy son, could really work full time. Almost the whole of the ex-wife's case rested on the inheritance (most of which was invested in the house the second wife was living in). Still, she succeeded in winning maintenance.

Muddled thinking surrounds this issue. No sooner did the Wilkinson case establish that an ex-wife could ask the court to order a second wife to file an affidavit of means than a judge in another case reported in *The Times* held that a third party, whether second wife or mistress, could not be ordered to, but might be cross-examined in court.

Writing in the *New Law Journal* in September 1980, Bernard Berkovits called for some clarification. He pointed out: 'The aim of the legislation (the Matrimonial Causes Act) is to achieve a just and fair division of the spouses' joint assets placing each of them as far as possible "in the financial position in which they would have been if the marriage had not broken down". But this cannot apply where new assets or sources of income become available to a spouse after (and usually because of) the breakdown of the marriage which would not have accrued had the marriage continued. Manifestly, this is the situation where such resources are provided by a new wife or mistress. To base assessment, therefore, on the notion that such resources free the husband's own means and should, therefore, enable the wife to obtain a larger share of them merely disguises the reality—that we are awarding the wife financial provision out of the assets of the husband's new wife or mistress.

'The assets of a new wife or mistress are not relevant to the financial claims of a former wife, irrespective of the way the rules or forms are drafted. Thus it should also be inadmissible to question a husband indirectly about the means of his new wife or mistress, or to take them into account even in a general way.'

What if you are not earning? Will an ex-wife automatically get less? Should you, for instance, give up work to have a baby, your husband may ask for his maintenance to be reduced because of changed circumstances. He may be lucky. On the other hand, he may be unlucky and have the amount raised because of inflation.

Perhaps the situation is best summed up by the present Lord Chancellor, Lord Hailsham, speaking to the House of Lords in a debate on the Matrimonial Homes Bill. 'The second wife has a pretty rough time. She has her legal rights. You can say to her, "Well, you knew what you were taking on when you married this man. You knew he had been married before. You knew he had four children." But she finds when she gets past the honeymoon that the first wife is constantly making applications to the court for the payment of maintenance, perhaps for the sale of what had been the matrimonial home and half the assets. She finds that she has to work for a living although she is bearing a series of children on the second marriage to the same man and she feels very hardly treated by the law. There has not been a word in this debate about that social situation, of which there are hundreds of thousands of cases going on at the present time.'

If your husband's ex-wife refuses to die ...

If your husband's ex-wife refuses to die, remarry, or support herself, what can you do about it? The short answer is not very much. But once you arrive at a settlement, the great thing is to stick to it. No weepy phone calls at two in the morning. 'Couldn't I have a few hundred pounds to go on holiday for a week or two?' For a start it will not be tax deductible—it could in reality be costing your husband something like twice that. And it is hardly fair on you. Money causes more trouble and strife in second marriages than all the other problems put together. You don't want to argue about it with your husband, because it puts your own marriage in jeopardy. But ex-wives frequently play on their husband's sympathies. And for purely logistical reasons ex-husbands often feel slightly guilty. In almost all divorces, the husband does the leaving, technically speaking. This puts him at an enormous psychological disadvantage. He half believes it when his ex-wife tells him how hard up she is. Remember, too, that husbands rarely leave home carrying washing machines, washing-up machines, vacuum cleaners or fanheaters under their arms when they go. Or carpets, or furniture or anything remotely useful. Until they come to replace these items they do not realize that their unclaimed share in consumer durables and hardware was worth a fortune, given a bit of inflation. His ex has all these things. But he has to buy them all over again.

Another favourite line of attack is to claim more money 'for the children'. This is very hard to refuse. A lot of men resent maintenance payments to their ex-wives, but are a great deal happier about shelling out for their kids. People come to crazy arrangements. One couple agreed all the terms of maintenance for the ex-wife and the children, with the proviso that 'large items of school uniform' would be paid for separately by the husband. They argued for weeks on end whether this meant large in size, large in price, or large in both every time one of the kids outgrew shoes or gymslips.

Many ex-wives are happy to shunt all financial responsibility for their children on to their husbands. They like to give the impression that unless little Johnny gets a brand new chopper bike this minute he will feel deprived, and end up a hooligan who beats up old ladies for fun. Fathers are often a soft touch—they want to be popular. And they are frightened of being cast as some old Scrooge who won't fork out any money. Look at it rationally. If dad was still at home would he buy a new chopper bike when a perfectly good second hand one was going round the corner for half the price? Would he jump to attention when his six-year-old demanded a £20 Tonka toy—or would he wait till Christmas or a birthday? Children are usually whole-hearted materialists, and many are strangely callous about playing on their parents' guilt complexes. It is far easier for a divorced father to spoil, rather than deprive, a child. Be suspicious of any vague demands 'for the children'. Buying a particular toy or financing a particular hobby is one thing, but if you are not careful you'll be contributing to a new three piece suite and carpet as well.

Education may be a problem. Perhaps little Johnny was put down for Winchester or Eton, or it was always assumed he would go to the local private school. He may even be there already—so it hardly seems fair to take him away. On top of everything else the fees could be crippling. So there is a great dilemma. Does your husband beggar himself and you to pay for it all or not? It is very difficult. You cannot help being influenced by the circumstances of divorce. If you lured him away from his wife and children, your conscience may nag sufficiently to let him reduce himself to threads and tatters on their behalf. But in the vast majority of cases, both sides are equally to blame for the divorce and its consequences. Inevitably, there is not so much money to spend on the children. What is his ex-wife prepared to contribute? Is she going to get a job to pay part of the school fees? If she is not prepared to work for her own kids, why should you be? And it may not be a good thing for the children to enjoy an expensive education beyond their parents' means. If everyone ends up poverty stricken on their behalf, perhaps they are going to feel guilty. If you have children of your own, is it fair to subsidize an education for his children that you know, given his obligations to his ex, you'll never be able to afford for your own?

Many ex-wives are not as badly off as they think they are. Or rather their ex-husbands and their second families might not be as well off as the ex-wife thinks they are. How your husband pays his maintenance may be as important as how much he pays.

Once a woman divorces she becomes responsible for paying her own tax. Some claim the system is too complicated and means that divorced women face large tax bills once or twice a year. The truth is that a divorced woman with a couple of children need not pay a penny of tax unless her income is nearly £5,000 a year. Middle class ex-wives can do rather well out of divorce. They benefit from the special concessions made to single-parent families, while having the good fortune to have divorced someone who can probably pay them as much in maintenance as the average working man earns.

The trick is to divide the maintenance so that the children can claim their own tax allowances. At the moment children's income is not aggregated by the taxman with the parents', so a child can receive up to £1,375 a year before tax is due. As long as the maintenance order is made out to the children personally (but clearly their mother is actually paid for them each month) they can claim their personal allowances. Divorced women with children are allowed the equivalent of the married man's tax allowance of £2,145. So the £4,895 can be distributed thus: £2,145 to the wife, £1,375 to each child. Result: she pays no tax on nearly £5,000 a year.

Far from the system discriminating against single-parent families, it can clearly favour them. A married man with a wife and two children earning the same amount would pay over £800 tax a year. And he wouldn't get the extra child benefit paid to single parents either.

Perhaps the best argument against maintenance is not that it is unfair on the second wife but that it is often unfair on the ex-wife as well. For the middle classes the financial aftermath of divorce may be crippling for ex-husbands; and ex-wives may get away with more than they should. A man who is in a professional job with an easily identified source of income, a house that he owns and perhaps a generous pension cannot escape the consequences. But lower down the income scale things are rather different. The man with an average wage packet cannot support two families. That is a fact of life. It is shown in the numbers of maintenance orders that are in arrears and the many single-parent families on supplementary benefits. This is why the one-parent family organizations have pressed for a guaranteed maintenance system funded largely by the state along the lines suggested by the Finer Committee rather than a 'get tough' policy with the husbands and fathers. None the less, the courts appear to operate on the unrealistic assumption that they should bend over backwards to extract money from a husband who cannot afford to pay rather than let an ex-wife live on social security where she would be as well, if not better, off. Second families fall between two stools. Firstly, they may be ignored by the courts. Secondly, they may find that the system of social security and the operation of the means test discriminates against them.

The courts have strange priorities. Aged judges railing against the irresponsibility of husbands sound as if they are at speech day in a Victorian workhouse. Some judges appear to regard themselves as the keepers of the public purse above all else. Dealing with low income families the courts have tended to the view that an ex-wife and children come first. A husband and a second family can be reduced to subsistence level by a maintenance order. In one case, Tovey v. Tovey, a husband's income was reduced below subsistence level by the court in order to impress him with his responsibility to his first family. In another a husband appealed against a maintenance order that left him £2 worse off than if he just gave up his job and drew supplementary benefit for himself and his new family. His argument was that the courts should use the 'liable relative' formula of the Supplementary Benefits Commission in evaluating how much he could afford to pay rather than the 'subsistence' assessment of the supplementary benefit rate used by the court. The 'liable relative' formula is supplementary benefit rate plus a quarter of the income and is used by the SBC to recoup money given to dependents. His plea failed but the order was reduced to leave him £1 a week better off than he would be by giving up his job.

But what seems to elude the courts is that an ex-wife on a low income can improve her position, but the ex-husband and his family who have been reduced to subsistence level cannot. The way the social security system operates, a second wife and her family can be far worse off than her predecessor. A single parent on supplementary benefit can earn a certain amount before her money is reduced. In effect 'subsistence' level should be assessed as supplementary benefit level plus that amount. She will be automatically entitled to other benefits—free dentistry and school meals for the children, plus rent or rate rebates or help in paying the interest on the mortgage. The ex-husband and his second family, who may be as badly off after maintenance payments, do not automatically qualify for such benefits. If he is working he cannot claim supplementary benefit—even if the income he has left is below that level. His ex-wife, however, may have her income made up to that amount. Family Income Supplement is the main support for low-income families where the husband is working, but maintenance payments cannot be taken off before claiming it unless the starting point was low enough. Rate and rent rebate rules are the same.

Mary Hayes, lecturer in the Faculty of Law at the University of Sheffield pointed out the impracticalities and injustices of this system in our divorce ridden era. 'It is suggested that a more understanding approach to poor men is desirable. A family which lives for long at subsistence level is put under considerable pressure, which may jeopardize its stability. Current principles fail to pay heed to the strain which is put on a second wife and children. Neither justice nor public policy are served if the effect of the court's order leads to the breakdown of the second family unit.'*

What it all boils down to is that the right hand of the courts doesn't know what the left hand of the Department of Health and Social Security is doing. The principles under which each of them operates are in many ways opposed. It is extremely difficult to persuade a court to abolish a maintenance order to an ex-wife on the grounds that she is living with another

* Tovey v. Tovey, 1978. See also *Supplementary Benefit and Financial Provision Orders* Mary Hayes BA, JP in *The Journal of Social Welfare Law,* May 1979.

man who is supporting her and being a husband in all but name. Yet the attitude to cohabitation taken by the DHSS is the reverse: a woman loses her benefit if she lets her boyfriend move in with her. She is immediately classified as his dependent. But if she was receiving maintenance, not social security, the situation is entirely different. She is still considered dependent on her first husband. Again, an ex-husband is not a 'liable relative' according to the Supplementary Benefits Commission who may pursue him for money to defray benefit paid for his children, but not his ex-wife. But as far as the divorce courts are concerned he is all too liable when it comes to supporting his ex-wife. The case for abolishing two conflicting sets of principles and establishing a Family Court to deal with all the matters stemming from divorce cannot be more compelling.

A Home of Contention

A HOUSE IS OFTEN a home of contention between divorcing couples, and no wonder. For most of us it is the biggest single investment we make in our lives. What with tax relief on the mortgage, and never-ending inflation, buying your own home has been an excellent investment. Half the families in the country are owner occupiers. What happens to their homes on divorce?

All is well if the proceeds of a sale are sufficient to buy two homes. But in many cases this is impossible: generally, though, divorcing couples are left without enough money to buy a house each. In the past wives often lost out when the house was in the husband's name. But nowadays a court will first see that the children of a broken marriage have a roof over their heads, regardless of who owns what. This is fine, but it poses considerable problems for husbands who want to remarry. Their capital may be tied up in the first home. They may be paying for the mortgage, making it difficult for them to take on another. A second wife might find the financial burden of putting a roof over her family's head rests largely on her. But more worrying than this is the growing tendency of the courts to give the husband's half share of the house to an ex-wife, even if there are no dependent children, as extra 'security'—in case he should stop maintenance payments—or even in lieu of the widow's pension she automatically loses the right to on divorce.

Divorce laws are to property rights what luck is to Monopoly

Divorce laws are to property rights what luck is to Monopoly. But when they pass GO divorced husbands cannot bank on collecting any money. An Englishman's home is no longer his castle, if he gets divorced.

Even twenty years ago property rights were sacrosanct. Now family law cheerfully overrules or ignores them. In the past wives were hard done by. Now they are protected. Back in the nineteenth century, before the Married Women's Property Act was passed, a wife could own no money or property of her own. Once she married it was her husband's. Even in the 1950s and 60s it was difficult for a wife to claim a share of the house on divorce unless it was in her name or owned jointly with her husband. Then it was established that the wife who could prove a financial contribution, directly, in the form of helping to pay the mortgage, financing improvements or indirectly by simply paying the food bills so enabling her husband to pay the mortgage, could get a share on divorce. But it was then argued, quite rightly, that the wife who gave up work to bring up a family is making a contribution, if not a financial one, to the family. Was it fair to exclude her? Of course not. As one judge put it the cock can feather the nest if he doesn't have to sit on it.

By the 1970s it was recognized that work done in the home, indeed the mere fact that a wife had lived and breathed in it for a number of years was to be considered sufficient 'contribution' under this definition. Moreover, the courts were given powers to transfer property between husband and wife. Nowadays an estimated three-quarters of married couples who buy their homes do so in joint names—but indeed such things matter little as far as divorce is concerned. It has become common for an ex-wife to be given not just a half share but the whole of the matrimonial home, and not just while the children are growing up. One wife claimed she had to continue to provide a home for her 26-year-old son. Joint ownership, or indeed any ownership is hardly worth the paper it is written on any more. Like everything else the pendulum has swung too far. A decade ago a divorced woman who did not own her home could be done out of her rightful share. Nowadays it is the husband who may never see the colour of his money again.

Divorcing owners of luxury mansions, 10 up 20 down, clearly have fewer problems. Houses like that can be sold and two homes bought for the price of one. Even if the husband is lumbered with maintenance payments at least he can get enough of his cash out to start again. The problems really emerge when the couple cannot agree on a reasonable division of the spoils. Or if the house is small or of just average value and could not realistically be expected to be divided.

If there are children the court will almost certainly order the home to be kept until they are grown up. A fashionable order used to be that it would be kept until the youngest child was 16 or 17 and then sold and the profits divided. This was thought to be quite a good way to get the husband to keep up his maintenance and mortgage payments—he would get his money in the end. The trouble was that children do not simply trot out of the house with a suitcase in hand as soon as they leave school. Even if they do, an ex-wife could go back to court claiming she had nowhere to live. Ex-wives have been allowed to snaffle their husband's share at the end of the day.

More commonly the wife may get the house and either she or her husband will be responsible for paying the mortgage. As far as the husband is concerned it might be better if his ex-wife is actually responsible for the mortgage if he has set his sights on buying another house with you. A single person, or a married couple cannot claim tax relief on mortgages of more than £25,000. If his name remains on the first mortgage for more than the 12 months concessionary period, and if the total of that and the new mortgage on any new home is over £25,000, you will lose tax relief.

If, on the other hand, he pays his ex maintenance out of which she is to pay the mortgage, he will get the normal tax relief on those payments. Unless he seriously believes that he is going to get his share of the house at the end of the day it would pay him to adopt the latter course.

Some couples have been known to split their homes in two—literally—if there was no way of selling it and providing a roof over both their heads. In one case an ex-wife and son lived in one part of the house, the ex-husband in the other. He was, apparently, much appreciated as a baby-sitter. But most second wives would not choose to start married life that way. Even moving into your husband's original home is fraught with problems and complications—psychological as well as financial. He may not be landed enough to have generations of gentry gazing from the walls, but it is very easy to feel a stranger in someone else's home.

Choosing somewhere to live together is one of the traditional treats of getting married. While he may count himself lucky to be left with the matrimonial home or have the opportunity and the money to buy his ex-wife out of her share, you may not be so overjoyed at the prospect of moving into what was, literally, her bed. It may be a mistake to move into his place. People who marry widows or widowers frequently find it difficult living with the past. The ghosts get distinctly rattled when a new husband or wife arrives. But even when the first wife is alive and still kicking her husband it can be quite intimidating.

Look before you leap. Once you have moved in it might be

The ghosts get distinctly rattled...

quite difficult to get him to consider another home and move out and you could be stuck forever in a house that will never be your home, no matter how well it suits you. If it offers plenty of room for improvement, you might be able to put your personal stamp on it. Often people live in the same place for years and just get used to eccentric plumbing and oddly patterned walls. In the end they just don't notice how awful it is any more. Perhaps he won't mind if the decorators move in before you do. It is easier to make your feelings known before you move in. You are hardly going to pack your bags and rush home to mother just because you can't stand the wallpaper.

How well you adapt to living in someone else's home depends partly on what you are used to. If you shared a flat or house before you married, it will seem sheer heaven not having to shift what seems like an entire underwear department every time you have a bath or wait until the television closes down before you can claim your bed in the communal sitting-room. But many single people nowadays like to buy a property before they get married—indeed as soon as they can scrape the deposit and mortgage payments together. And if you are used to having a place of your own you might find it more difficult to settle down in his. It really rather depends on his attitude. He may love the idea of someone leaping in with their paints, wallpapers and Black and Decker workbench to bring some light into his life and dark corners. Or he may not.

Some men simply do not notice what their womenfolk do with the insides of their houses—unless they come home to find the walls down, or a swimming-pool where the patio used to be. Many are content to let their wives make up their minds for them when it comes to the curtains and carpets. You may even in time be able to remove discreetly any item that fills you with particular horror. But if he fancies himself as David Hicks watch out.

It might be better then to start in a new house. Then it will be *our* house not *his*. But selling is an upheaval and often an expensive one. Solicitors' fees, stamp duty, estate agents' commission all add up to a lot of money—£2,000 or more. If you can stand it, forgo the pleasures and pains of househunting—it is always a more difficult business when you have a home to sell—there are distinct advantages in staying put.

What if he needs to raise some cash to buy out his ex-wife? If you are earning you will probably want to help out. If you can do so, it gives you a good opportunity to have a stake in the house—which you would want to have anyway.

This is an area fraught with complications. If you are not careful the extra money you borrow will not qualify for mortgage interest relief. Some years ago, when second homes were all the rage, legislation was brought in to prevent people enjoying tax relief on loans for any property that was not their main residence. One of the loopholes closed up was the situation where someone could get a second mortgage on his other home and then hop off and buy a little rural retreat with, of course, the payments attracting tax relief. Another gap in the defences was plugged by the rule that husband and wife could not expect tax relief on any loans made for the purpose of transferring property between each other. An unforseen side-effect of this was to complicate life for couples who are property owners in their own right before marriage.

There is no problem about buying out an ex-wife or husband. That satisfies the Inland Revenue's criterion that a genuine sale and purchase has been made. The loan raised to buy one partner out will qualify for tax relief because this purchaser is increasing his or her interest in the property. The trouble comes when wife or husband number two is raising the money to buy a share from their new spouse. It pays to raise the loan and convey the half share of the house to you before you get married. If you do it after you are married the new money you have raised as husband and wife will not attract mortgage interest relief.

Of course, if you are borrowing money to undertake improvements—put in central heating or build an extension—this entitles you to tax relief. And if you buy your share direct from the ex-wife that will be all right too, whether you are married or not. It is only if you want to raise money to buy a share from your intended that the problem arises.

There are other property complications for remarriers. Most newly-married couples find that they don't have enough of anything—re-marriers might find they have too much, particularly when it comes to houses. The key point is that individuals on their own may claim tax relief on loans of up to £25,000 on their main residence. But a married couple is allowed only the same amount, not double. So what happens if one or both partners are property owners but wish either to move into one of the homes or buy something completely different? Suppose they cannot sell their house, or houses, fast enough. There are special tax concessions for this situation. Where one goes to live in the other's house for a year after the move, he or she can continue to receive full tax relief on his or her original loan. Where two people want to sell to move into a third property, the same principle applies. Although married they can enjoy tax relief on the original loans for a year from the date of the new loan. For that period they will have two lots of £25,000 limits, not one as is usually the case with married couples.

Joint ownership is a thorny topic in remarriages where one partner is moving into the other's home. The vast majority of married couples nowadays buy their first home together. They are both earning. They pool their resources. There is no argument or difficulty. But should a second wife expect to get half shares in her husband's house when she marries him? Quite clearly he has contributed far more to it financially than she has. He may have bought it years ago and the mortgage may be a fraction of its value now. Should she expect to be a joint owner? Many divorced men are rather cagey about extending joint ownership in these circumstances, largely because they worry about the possibility of another divorce and losing half their assets again. The fact is that as far as divorce is concerned ownership does not mean a great deal—but there are good reasons why married couples, and especially remarried couples should own their house jointly.

The most common form of joint ownership is a joint tenancy. This does not mean half shares. It means that together you own the whole. On the death of one, the survivor automatically takes over the lot. This is particularly important if there is an ex-wife or other dependents around who might make a claim on his estate if, perish the thought, he should pop off unexpectedly. You cannot leave your portion of a joint tenancy to anyone in your will. It is taken over by the surviving spouse, so it is safe in the event of any claims being made on your money after you have gone. Well, almost safe, (see Chapter 8, *Where There's a Will...*)

Joint tenancy, however, may not suit the circumstances of a second or subsequent marriage. There may be children from a previous relationship to whom the divorced father, or indeed mother, wants to bequeath a share of his or her assets. A second wife may find it hard to accept that she would have to sell her home on the death of her husband. And if she had children she would be foolish to do so. One solution to the question of joint ownership or to ownership at all might be to become tenants in common. Far less widely used than a joint tenancy, this arrangement means that each partner has a specific share in the house that can, for instance, be left to someone in a will.

Be warned. Acquiring a share in his property can be an

expensive business. For transactions of £20,000 or more, stamp duty becomes payable on an upwards sliding scale, depending on the amounts involved. Fortunately, this imposition should affect only fairly expensive houses. In the case of conveying a house into joint ownership the size of the transaction would be taken as half the market value of the house minus half the borrowing on it. So a house with a value of £60,000, and a £20,000 mortgage would be considered to have some £40,000 worth of equity. One half of that, £20,000, would slip in at the bottom of the stamp duty scale. The tax on that transaction would be £100. However, if the house had a £25,000 mortgage the equity value would be only £35,000 and so the conveyance of half that amount would not suffer stamp duty. So long as the cost is not a problem—and with most houses it should not be—the argument for putting your husband's home into joint names when you marry is a strong one. If you contribute to its cost and upkeep you have a right to expect your efforts to be recognized officially. After all, he could probably not afford to live somewhere as nice—or repair somewhere as dilapidated—if he didn't have you to share the expenses.

In the present daft state of the law, a wife who is divorcing seems to have more rights to the house she lives in than one who is happily married. Many divorced husbands find themselves in bedsitters. To add insult to injury some have found that the fact that they haven't 'proper homes' is sometimes given by ex-wives as a reason to restrict access to the children.

But perhaps you are the partner with property. Should you let him move in with you? No sooner does he decide to divorce than he arrives on your doorstep clutching his teddy bear and toothbrush and asking for shelter. But it may not be wise to permit him permanent official residence until the details of his divorce are settled. If he is living in the home of a second wife or mistress he may be reducing his claim, in the eyes of the court, to a share in his original house. Frequently the fact that a man is living with a girlfriend is offered as proof that a husband doesn't 'need' his share of the house.

It may be that his case is stronger if he argues from a position of weakness. If a second wife or girlfriend is providing him with a home he might not find the court so sympathetic. It is all too easy for an ex-wife and her solicitors to seize on the fact that he has moved into your Mayfair penthouse as an excuse for denying him a share of what is rightfully his. While most husbands accept that the children should stay in their home, even if it means their ex-wives having exclusive use of the hard-earned G-Plan, few can see why the lot should be transferred to her forever. The courts increasingly regard the husband's share of the marital home as extra 'security' for an ex-wife, even if she has no children. Professional men in their forties are probably the worst hit. If they have a good salary it is assumed that they can simply start all over again.

The fact that he is living with a second wife or mistress might, in the eyes of the court, reduce his 'need' for a share in the matrimonial home. The courts do not seem to inquire very deeply into whether the relationship that is supplying the roof over a man's head is permanent. There have been cases where men in bedsitters and short-life housing with no dependent children have been informed that they do not 'need' their share of the family house because they are already housed.

If, at the end of the day, you are faced with the prospect of having to start from scratch in the housing market because he and his ex-wife cannot agree on sharing the assets, what should you do?

Most building societies will offer a customer around two and a half times their annual income by way of a loan for house buying. Sometimes you might get three times. Essentially the building society is interested in fixing its level of borrowing so that the customer will not have difficulty in meeting the repayments. A man earning £8,000 a year, for instance, might be considered good for a loan of £20,000—two and a half times his income.

If he is paying £2,000 maintenance a year that clearly affects his ability to pay and it is a foolish house buyer and building society that does not take that into account. But if you are earning a reasonable salary it may make sense for you to be the principal borrower. As a rule you will be able to raise more money jointly if your earnings are more than his after deducting his maintenance payments. The Sex Discrimination Act prevents building societies turning up their noses at the wife as breadwinner.

But when couples apply on the basis of joint incomes they are not given two and a half times their joint salaries. The higher earner may get two and a half times and to that may be added the equivalent of one year of the secondary income. A man earning around £8,000 a year and paying £2,000 in maintenance would be able to raise a mortgage of around £15,000. If his second wife was earning £8,000 as well they might jointly get £23,000. But if she put her salary forward as the main one she would obtain perhaps £20,000—two and a half times her income, plus perhaps £6,000 extra on the joint basis—£26,000 in all.

Where There's a Will...

HIS MONEY NEVER becomes him in life the leaving of it all to you when he goes. But second wives may be unmerry widows if they are not careful. Even where he has made a will in your favour, his ex-wife may well have her way with it. You might be under the impression that a man's obligations to his ex-wife die with him. Not so. Before you can chant '*Requiescat in Pace*', there will be a solicitor's letter on the doormat demanding a share of the loot. Soon you'll discover a whole new meaning to the phrase 'dear departed'.

People do not like to think about death. Usually this attitude does little lasting harm. Unless they are Howard Hughes or Paul Getty, making a will should be a straightforward matter. For most the major asset is the family home and that is usually inherited automatically by the survivor. Most of us do not expect our passing to be of much financial interest to anyone else.

But life—or death—is not such a simple matter for second wives. They could easily find themselves beggared by paying off the first wife. Their husbands may dutifully leave them everything, but the first wife has the legal right to take a large slice of it away again.

The Inheritance (Provision for Family and Dependents) Act 1975 takes over where the divorce laws leave off. You may

. . . but you may unwittingly have made a more lasting contract with his ex-wife

marry your husband 'til death you do part, but you may unwittingly have made a more lasting contract with his ex-wife. If he was paying his ex-wife maintenance and she has not remarried, she might well have a claim on his estate. It is not unknown for a court to award an ex-wife half of the estate even when the husband thought he had left the lot to his second wife. The implications of the inheritance laws are enough to make a man turn in his grave—or be buried in it like the Egyptian Kings with all his wordly goods stacked around him.

The road to hell is paved with good intentions. Inheritance laws are to protect people who may be badly treated under someone's will. But they have been misused so that ex-wives can still cause upset and mischief when their ex-husbands die.

The laws were originally designed to stop potty old eccentrics leaving their riches to Battersea Dogs Home and their widows and children in poverty. Or to dissuade philanderers of more modest means giving the family semi to the latest mistress. The inheritance laws take most of the point, not to mention the fun, out of any dramatic deathbed decisions to cut your scandalous eldest son out of your will or ignore your daughter because she married beneath her. As soon as you pop off, they can go to the court and try to get a share. Husbands or wives can claim money from a dead spouse's estate if they think they have been hard done by. If there was no will, for instance, and the estate was fairly large, a survivor might find that the intestacy provisions do not leave them a big enough slice.

But under the more recent law, anyone who can show they were dependent on the person who died may have a claim. The result has been vast numbers of frivolous applications as a steady stream of clandestine mistresses, housekeepers, stable girls and kennel maids have crept out of the woodwork to claim a share of their dead 'friend's' estate. Many cases are settled out of court, to avoid a public scandal. And because the costs of fighting are so high, settling is often considered the cheapest solution—and the most discreet.

Second wives rarely realize that they could be at risk if their husband's ex-wife has not remarried. Even if he was not paying maintenance, she could still have a claim. It is not just a law that affects the rich. A widowed second wife may not be safe in her own home unless it is entirely in her name. And the courts tend to be as generous to ex-wives after their husband's death as they were when he was alive.

One second wife was left £50,000 when her husband died. She had a twelve-year-old daughter at boarding school. Her husband had not lived with his first wife for over twenty years.

... a steady stream of clandestine mistresses, housekeepers, stable girls and kennel maids have crept out of the woodwork ...

His other children were the same age as the second wife. His ex-wife claimed and got £10,000 out of his estate in an out-of-court settlement. The widow was advised by her solicitors to settle. The case had already dragged on for two and a half years and the costs, which were paid out of the estate (further reducing what she had left) were over £7,000. While all this was going on she had little to live on. The money was frozen and she had to beg for something to get by on. Her daughter had to be taken away from her school. Joint bank accounts could not be used. Fortunately the house was in her name, otherwise the eventual settlement on the ex-wife might have been even higher.

Perhaps that second wife would have been better off going to court. Very few of the thousands of claims made each year get as far as the law courts, so the Inheritance and Dependents Act has not been fully tested. But it's of little comfort. In one case the judge awarded an ex-wife £7,000, half the husband's estate. It had all been left to the second wife. The claimant had divorced her husband seventeen years ago, and she was only two years older than the widow. It seems that any ex-wife who has not re-married and was receiving maintenance has a good case. If his maintenance agreement states that he pays her until the death of one or the other of them, do not be fooled. It does not mean she cannot claim your money after he has gone. Clearly the circumstances dictate how much she would get but even small amoints of money that would hardly keep one widow in comfort are split to give the ex-wife something.

Most husbands are oblivious to this. They think that if they have paid up generously during their lifetime, that is enough. But the more maintenance he paid when alive, the more she is likely to be able to claim after his death. Even if the maintenance agreement includes a provision that neither party will make a claim on the other's death, this has never been tested in law. Many lawyers think that such a provision would make no difference.

Husbands are not, as a rule, overkeen to leave money to their ex-wives unless they have young children or cash to spare. They usually feel their ex has extracted quite enough from them during their life without making further capital after their death. Most people are hard pushed to provide for the wives they leave behind them, let alone worry about the ones who may have left them behind. Most just do not realize how an ex-wife can appropriate their widow's money once they are gone. The powers of the Inheritance Act are positively Draconian. They can overrule the intestacy provisions which are used for carving up an estate if someone dies leaving no will. Normally these rule that the widow gets the first £40,000, half the rest goes to the children, and the other half becomes theirs on their mother's death.

Under the old inheritance laws your husband could simply have signed all his loot over to you on his death bed. You could receive his stocks and shares, his numbered Swiss bank accounts or just his humble building society savings immediately before he popped off, and that was too bad for everyone else.

Under the 1975 Act, any such dodges to avoid a claim on the estate can be unscrambled by the courts unless they were done a full 6 years before death. Another feature of the latest Act is the new definition of 'net estate'. Usually 'net estate' excludes any asset or property held jointly. Many married couples own their houses as joint tenants. On the death of one, the other automatically inherits the rest. That half by-passes the estate. You cannot leave your share to anyone else or will it to the cat. All sorts of other assets, like bank accounts and insurance policies can be held in this way. But when it comes to the 1975 Inheritance Act, the court can order that half a house or a bank account held jointly can be included in the 'net estate', to be added in and shared out as it sees fit.

In the rules of this elastic Act, the claims of ex-spouses are treated as they are in the financial provisions of the Matrimonial Causes Act, 1973. This means the court can consider such things as the length of the marriage, the needs and wherewithal of the beneficiaries, conduct and prospects—the same things, in fact, as when an application for maintenance is made.

No one knows how far a court would go to provide for an ex-wife. If the only asset was a house and the ex already has one, can a widow be forced to sell? The court certainly has the power to force her to, by making cash demands to pay the ex-wife. A second wife who worked for a living may have less of a case than an ex-wife who had just lived off the husband. The Act helps those who do not help themselves to help themselves to other people's money. Some widows pay off their husbands' ex-wives by making over monthly amounts out of their capital, in the hope that the old girl will conveniently expire. Others find they have to part with the cash.

In one case the judge gave an ex-wife half the estate—which had been left to the second wife. Both women were in their mid-fifties. In another, the judge thought it reasonable that an ex-wife should expect the same maintenance after her former husband's death as she received when he was alive.* The widow's inheritance, adding up to around £36,000 including the value of the house, had to provide £1,000 a year maintenance to the ex-wife. The fact that the money had been accumulated since the end of the first marriage did not affect the issue.

The worst feature of the Act is that it gives ex-wives a second bite at the cherry. When they divorce, they have a chance to stake their claim to a share of the spoils. They may get half of everything, and a house into the bargain. The Inheritance Act lets them come back for a slice of the capital their husbands have built up since the split, entirely by their own and their second wife's efforts.

There is a large element of blackmail, too. An ex-wife who has received maintenance usually has a good claim, and her solicitors can be confident she will get something. The beneficiaries of the estate know it, too, or their advisers will. If the case goes to court and the claimant gets something, costs will be awarded against the estate, adding the insult of legal bills to the injury of parting with the cash. If the claim fails, the widow or whoever benefited from the estate will probably have to pay their own costs—and if the judge thinks the claim, even

* Re Eyre 1968

though it failed, was 'meritorious' the claimant's expenses might come out of the estate as well. Either way you lose. Moreover, the first £2,500 of anything awarded is ignored when deciding what the successful claimant should pay for legal aid.

Prevention is better than cure. How do you avoid the 1975 Inheritance Act? Quite clearly a divorced man who has remarried should strive to die a pauper. Anyone paying an ex-wife might think this is the easiest thing in the world. But many of us nowadays die quite rich, by the time houses and pensions are brought into account.

A second wife may expect to be a widow for far longer than a first wife. In second marriage, the age gap tends to be wider. On average, women live around 7 years longer than men, although that period may be shortening as more women smoke, drink and go out to work. Still, it is probable that your widowhood could be a lengthy one if your husband is 10 or more years older than you.

At the very least, your husband should instruct his solicitor to make a will. Any existing wills are invalidated by his remarriage (though divorce does not automatically change things). People are notoriously superstitious about wills. Every day of the week perfectly sensible husbands and fathers drop dead with coronaries, leaving their affairs in a muddle. Businessmen spend their lives keeping the odd pence in the pound out of the clutches of the taxman, but seem happy to give up the ghost plus the maximum capital transfer tax when they die.

Suggest your husband makes a will and he might think you will lace his tea with arsenic or run him down accidentally on purpose in the drive. Like some megalomaniac millionaire he might worry that the entire family is waiting for him to pass away so they can get their hands on his golf clubs or premium bonds. Get an outsider he trusts to make him see that everyone should make a will. If we were able to come back to life, most of us would be pleasantly, or perhaps not so pleasantly, surprised to see what we were worth. And even if you think the intestacy provisions cover the amounts you may be left, it is far easier for a family to get hold of whatever modest sum might be available if there is a will. You may have to wait months if he dies without one.

Most husbands leave the lot to their widows, or divide it between their widows and their children. If he has children from a first marriage who are still at school, or at any rate not earning their living, he should provide some income for them if he can. Only the well-heeled have large amounts of loose cash lying around, so it might not be practical for him to will a few thousand to his children. Perhaps his only asset is his share in the house. He wants to protect this for you. The best solution would be for him to take out a family income benefits policy specifically for his children, written in trust for them, which would provide income for a number of years if he should die.

If his children are grown up and the only likely claimant not left anything is the ex-wife, then he should try to keep as much of his money outside his 'net estate' as possible. What he leaves out of his will is far more important than what he puts in. Anything held in joint names, for instance, becomes automatically the property of the survivor when the other dies. Under the amended laws a court can take a dead person's half into account. But putting it in joint names means that only half and not the whole of the value could be within possible claiming distance of his ex-wife.

Take the home you live in, the most important asset of all. If he dies owning it and willing it to you, there is no guarantee that you will be able to keep it. It will be part of his net estate, and might account for a great deal of it. If his ex-wife makes a claim, you might be forced to sell it in order to pay her. If it is some ramshackle terrace with an outside lavatory, but all you have in the world, the court might be sympathetic, since paying her would see you destitute. But, if it could be shown that you could sell up and buy yourself something cheaper, releasing some cash for her, a court might well ask you to do exactly that. Whether you live in a lean-to or a palace, why should you run the risk of losing your home when your husband dies?

Make him see that he must put the house in joint names so

your half share will not fall into his net estate. You will inherit the lot automatically. Even then, you will not be 100% safe. The court can order his half to be added into his estate. Supposing he left you a house worth £100,000 but a net estate worth hardly anything, and an ex-wife who wanted some money. In that situation a court might well consider that his half of the house should be included. Unless you had some spare cash, you might have to sell to pay her.

Better still you could have everything put in your name. What if your husband is panic stricken at the thought of giving it all away, or worried that you will boot him out the minute it is yours? He could give it to you, but have a life interest for himself. Then he cannot be turned out, and the place cannot be sold without his consent. So long as you do this 6 years before he dies, no one can touch you once he has gone. He can make the same sort of arrangement with other assets—cash, stocks and shares, even his antique furniture—if he wants. It is worth spending a few hours with a solicitor getting it sorted out.

With so much divorce, dodging the inheritance laws could take over where the tax avoidance industry leaves off. Indeed, the measures taken to avoid ex-wives are often identical to those which thwart the taxman.

The key principle is that your husband should die owning nothing. Only assets that he is free to dispose of are included in a will or counted for capital transfer tax. Many life insurance policies, for instance, are written in trust for a particular person, often a wife or child. If the person whose life was insured dies, the proceeds go direct to the person named as beneficiary on the insurance policy and are not included in the estate. Some people do not bother to name a specific beneficiary, and just write a will disposing of whatever cash is there including insurance payments. If the lot is going to a wife anyway, there will be no capital transfer tax because gifts or legacies made within a marriage are exempt. But the insurance cash will still count in the estate—and this is the danger for second wives. There is no tax, but an ex-wife may be able to claim part of it unless it is written in trust for you or your children.

A court cannot bust a trust—or so it is thought. The most it can do is order the last 6 years' premiums to be paid back. If a life policy was taken out just a few years, or even a few months, before death, the court can probably only claw back the premiums, but not the benefit if it was written in trust for widow or children. It would be difficult, if not impossible, for the court to prove that a life policy had been written so as to avoid a claim on someone's estate. Most insurance companies encourage their clients to write policies in trust because it saves them trouble when it comes to dishing out the cash.

As a formerly married man, he might be up to his ears in insurance policies already. Take a look at them. Sometimes the beneficiary is simply named 'the wife'. Do not worry if he took out the policy years before he even clapped eyes on you. The wife in question is the one he has when he dies, not the one he had when he took it out. Insurance policies frequently escape the beadiest-eyed ex-wife. She is usually far too busy arguing about the family silver, the house or the three piece suite. A piece of paper is less obvious and once you have married him, this becomes your policy.

What if a policy written in trust for his ex is discovered at the bottom of a drawer one day? Or the insurance company writes asking why the premiums haven't been paid on a policy everyone had forgotten?

If his ex-wife has forgotten about it, she might treat it as a welcome windfall, and split the proceeds with him. But if she is named as the beneficiary, it is technically hers (even if your hubby coughs up the premiums). If it is an endowment or some form of savings-linked policy, it will have a surrender value. If it is just ordinary life cover, with no savings element, it will be worth nothing until your husband, whose life it covers, pops off. Unless it has been written in trust specifically for his ex-wife, the premiums should be paid. It is probably cheaper than reinsuring him now. But if it is definitely for his ex-wife's benefit because she is named, should he carry on with the payments on her behalf? You could abandon the policy, giving her the surrender value. Or consider carrying it on as a way of making sure she has some sort of lump sum if he should die. Then she could not claim she was destitute, and this could help cut the chances of any claim she might want to make against the estate.

Divorced wives on maintenance are frequently advised to take out a policy on their ex-husbands' lives anyway. But it might be better if he took out one for her. There was a case where a divorced woman received capital, a house, and maintenance on divorce. A year later, the husband died. He had agreed to pay her extra maintenance to cover the cost of a life insurance policy to benefit her if he died, thinking this would pre-empt a claim to the money he left his long-standing mistress. But after he died the ex-wife made a claim: though she had agreed to she had not taken out the insurance policy.

The trouble with trying to dodge the Inheritance Act is that money or whatever has to be given away much sooner than it really should be. It is all very well for a second wife to get the home, the endowment policies and the kitchen sink in her name. But if you should die first, you might have left it all to your children. You may make a will as your part of the bargain, but you can change a will without letting anyone know. And that sparks off these gruesome deathbed squabbles between supposed heirs and lady 'companions' about whether the old buffer had lost his marbles when he willed away his oil wells. Setting up a trust or settlement for someone else means that the person doing the giving must lose all rights and benefits of the money. There's no going back for him if wife number two—you—ran off with the milkman.

Gifts between husband and wife, before or after death, are tax-exempt, but a well-heeled father who wants to dish out cash to the kids has to be careful not to fall foul of capital transfer tax. Awareness of this helps explain how many wealthy men can die so modestly. For lesser mortals it is clearly impossible to afford the luxury of the whizz-kid advisers who deal with the very rich. But your solicitor should know about trusts and tax—and if he doesn't he will know an accountant who does. With so much divorce about, the insurance companies are well aware of the problems. Any company or insurance broker should be able to advise you on the best policies to buy.

Try as he may to die a pauper, your husband may not feel like turning all his wordly goods over to you. So instead of leaving cash around in bank accounts, or even in stocks and shares, he might consider what is delicately known as alternative investment. Books, stamps, Persian carpets, maps, even Victorian biscuit tins are now big business for collectors, along with the well established antiques and conventional art markets. Alternative investment has become fashionable partly because most of these items avoid tax. They are classed as 'chattels'. Any profit they make only attracts capital gains tax when the sale price is over £2,000. And that covers 95% of saleroom lots. And investments like rare stamps and jewellery are also attractive because they are easily transportable. It can even be difficult to trace the whereabouts of Chippendale chairs or Louis XV bureaux. Not to put too fine a point on it, these 'chattels' are a good way of storing money in a discreet way.* And because they can be insured against theft or damage, with the chance of rising in value, they are safer and more rewarding than cash losing real value under the mattress or in a hole at the bottom of the garden.

What about his pension? When you marry him, this may be the last thing on your mind. But some men have found their mink-lined pension benefits prevent them even getting divorced. It is not unknown for a judge to refuse a divorce after five years' separation if the wife is getting on a bit and claims that loss of the widow's pension when he dies will mean severe financial hardship.

And it is quite common for the ex-wife to try and squeeze some extra capital or his share in the house out of the husband to replace the pension she stands to lose. Courts have ordered

* Alternative investments are low profile assets (what the Italians call *Bene di Rifugio*) whose ownership and whereabouts is not usually on public record. There is no doubt that the payment of Capital Transfer Tax on many such assets is widely regarded as optional.' Robin Duthy, *Alternative Investment*

some ex-husbands who are nearing retirement age to buy annuities out of their capital to provide a substitute for the widow's pension when they go. The lump sum involved may be considerable, and few can afford it. The real problems come when people in their fifties or sixties divorce. But these days, when index-linked pension benefits may be worth their weight in gold, and most of us are in some sort of contributory scheme, it may well become a worry for those in their forties, or even younger. Pension benefits, in fact, could be the single biggest plum in a man's financial pie. Fortunately, the courts have no powers to alter payments of cash or income to the rightful widow. We have not adopted the system which forces widows in some countries to split their pension with any number of former wives, according to the length of each marriage. Over here, it is different. A man's widow's complete pension falls into the lap of the wife he was married to when he died, even if she had only been married to him for five minutes, and the ex-wife had to put up with him for fifty years.

It is not really as open to abuse as you might think. The thought of having to put up with some grumpy, albeit wealthy, geriatric for decades longer than expected is probably enough to deter the most ardent gold-digger. None the less, the rules on widow's pensions are rather out of step with the first come, first served attitude normally taken towards ex-wives. This has not gone unremarked. The Occupational Pensions Board, which vets company schemes, once suggested to the government that the courts be given powers to divide up the widow's pension among various wives. The Law Commission rejected the idea.*

The central point is that, since a man cannot give away his widow's pension in his will, it is not something that can be claimed by anyone else. And the same goes for lump sum benefit bestowed by the pension fund. Since it is not something the man can control, it is not counted as part of his

* It was considered 'too great a burden to expose the trustees of a pension fund who can be confidently expected to act conscientiously to the scrutiny of the court'. Law Commission Report Family Provision on Death, paragraph 213.

estate. He cannot leave his widow's pension to his secret mistress. The widow alone is entitled to a widow's pension.

Because of the spread and improvement of pension schemes in recent years, many of us are worth far more dead than alive. Quite apart from the widow's pension, usually half the normal retirement pension, there could be cash to come from a pension fund when a husband dies before retirement age. Since this is likely to be anything from twice to four times a man's annual salary, it is not to be sniffed at. But it may be up for grabs by his ex-wife. Pension funds do not automatically pay it to the widow. It is usually claimable by 'dependents', who are defined by the precise wording of the pension fund's trust deed. Each pension fund is a law unto itself on this—and there are over 60,000 different occupational schemes If the ex-wife dons her widow's weeds and sidles round to see the trustees declaring her poverty, they may consider giving her a slice of the action. Many pension funds ask their employees to nominate who they would like to get the goodies when they go. The technical term is 'to express a wish', and your husband should obviously do this. It is not legally binding on the trustees—otherwise the money would be treated as the employee's and taxed and included in his estate. But it gives them a guide.

A second wife should make some enquiries into her husband's pension scheme. And not just the one he is in now, but others that he may have contributed to in some previous employment. A man who changes jobs may well have what is known as a deferred pension, or even a number of them, which he may draw when he retires from the pension fund of a previous employer. But, if he was not married to you at the time he worked there, you may not be entitled to the widow's pension—nobody will be. You must look at the fine print of the trust deeds. If he is coasting along secure in the thought that you are well provided for, perhaps he should take a closer look and some advice on the subject.

With so much divorce and remarriage it can be difficult for the pension fund trustees, too. When the funds talk of 'dependents', they must use their discretion in, for instance, dividing money between two sets of children. One pension fund was amazed when the liftman, who had lost a leg in the war, died. No fewer than three mistresses popped up to claim his pension.

There are pitfalls galore in inheritance and it pays to plan ahead. But do not let your husband kill himself in his efforts to die a pauper—the best laid plans of mice, men and second wives, can be ruined by an unexpected turn of events. The wrong person dies first, or the tax man dreams up some new rules. So keep it simple. Make sure the house you live in is secure. Check that any insurance is written in trust for the intended beneficiary. Keep your money separate from your husband's. Be certain you can lay claim to half his cash by holding it in a joint account.

And may you live happily ever after.

Be certain you can lay claim to . . . his cash